To Doris,

Best Personal Wishes,

Tom Mullen

Birthdays, Holidays, and Other Disasters

Birthdays, Holidays, and Other Disasters

Thomas Mullen

Abingdon Press
Nashville — New York

To my mother and father

Preface

In times like these, can a book of humorous meditations be justified? In a world beset by problems that threaten to consume us and plagued by trivia which get in the way of their solution, is there really a place for a book carrying the unlikely title of *Birthdays, Holidays, and Other Disasters?*

We think so, primarily for the following reason:

Way down deep, there is a need for shallowness. From time to time we need to be reminded that we take ourselves too seriously and that seeing the humor of our situation enables us to keep both our problems and our achievements in perspective. Both to make this point and to add some class to the book, we have included a quotation from Reinhold Niebuhr, who never has been accused of failing to take the problems of the twentieth century seriously enough.

I am grateful to Gordon Thompson of the Earlham College English Department, whose genuinely clever and profound speech at an Earlham convocation in 1969 provided inspiration and considerable content for the meditation entitled "On Turning 30." Its inclusion should teach him to be more careful in the future about copyrighting his material.

I am grateful, too, for the good eyesight and diligent efforts of Doris Burkhart, Marie Foreman, Helen Liebert, and Dorthea Toney, who typed and retyped the manuscript for the book. Each deserves a better fate than trying to read my writing and a greater reward than words of thanks for their hard work.

My wife, Nancy, our four children, and the dog merit substantial recognition, too, as much of this book is autobiographical. We have shared a number of birthdays and holidays and a great many other disasters together. Nancy read the entire manuscript and thought it was great, an opinion which, unfortunately, must be considerably discounted because she loves the author very much, a fact which brings him joy whether the book succeeds or not.

My brother, Frank, made a number of suggestions about the book, few of which were adopted as they were irrelevant. However, he always buys lots of copies and gives them to his friends, and for this I am most grateful.

Lastly, and probably to my mother's great surprise, many thanks are extended to my parents, Albert and Bernice Mullen. My father, who died while this book was in its earliest stages, demonstrated a joy in living which manifested itself in a delightful sense of humor. He taught us not to take life too seriously. My mother taught us to take it seriously enough, to see our obligations and duties in life. Something of each of them is in this book, and to them it is dedicated with love.

TOM MULLEN

Laughter is a sane and healthful response to the innocent foibles of men; and even to some which are not innocent. All men betray moods and affectation, conceits and idiosyncrasies, which could become the source of great annoyance to us if we took them too seriously. It is better to laugh at them....

Humour is a proof of the capacity of the self to gain a vantage point from which it is able to look at itself. The sense of humour is thus a by-product of self-transcendence. ... All of us ought to be ready to laugh at ourselves because all of us are a little funny in our foibles, conceits and pretensions. What is funny about us is precisely that we take ourselves too seriously. We are rather insignificant little bundles of energy and vitality in a vast organization of life. But we pretend that we are the very center of this organization. This pretension is ludicrous; and its absurdity increases with our lack of awareness of it. The less we are able to laugh at ourselves the more it becomes necessary and inevitable that others laugh at us.

Reinhold Niebuhr in Holy Laughter

Contents

On the Birth of a First Child

Many jokes have been made about the distraught father-to-be pacing the floor, waiting anxiously for the birth of his child. Indeed, in literature and the movies the expectant father is usually portrayed as a chain-smoking, neurotic, unkempt, ridiculous buffoon, totally without understanding of the biological phenomenon which is taking place.

In reality, of course, this picture is not accurate, as many fathers do not smoke. Furthermore, the extent to which the other elements of the caricature are valid is determined largely by the manner in which the father is treated by that great institution of mercy and healing, your friendly hospital.

Do not misunderstand: the modern hospital usually treats pregnant women with enormous quantities of tender, loving care. Wives are comfortably located in modern rooms with private baths and often telephones. For a small charge they can enjoy cultural murder mysteries and comforting world news on their own television sets. A bevy of pleasant and well-starched nurses respond in double time whenever a tiny button is pushed. Maternity wards are usually happy places to be, too, and just right for having babies.

Consider, however, the plight of the expectant father. Three floors below the delivery rooms is a waiting room into which every bewildered and anxious father-to-be is ushered and where he is left to suffer and answer questions about how "the little wife" is doing. Of course, he doesn't really know how she's doing because no one tells him anything. The doctor knows, the nurses know, even the fellow who mops the floor knows, but the would-be father only knows that he does not know. Every so often a man with a white coat pops in and says "chin up," but few hospitals take seriously the fact that the husband might be slightly curious about whether or not he's a father. For all he knows, he may be in the wrong hospital.

Perhaps there is, however, method in this madness. Perhaps those modern benches in that waiting room which are too short to sleep on, too wide to sit on, too lumpy to stand on, and too fragile to lean against are just to prepare a man for the coming rigors of two o'clock feedings. Furthermore, it is for reasons of consistency that there are seldom magazines, books, newspapers, or calendars to read. Clearly, the room is for *waiting*, not reading.

We take that back. There are usually three items available for reading. One will be a pamphlet put out by some sectarian group, wanting to know where we are going to spend eternity. (After twelve or fourteen hours of waiting, most expectant fathers think they know the answer.) Another brochure you can expect to find will explain how you can go about leaving money to the hospital—if you have any left after paying your bill. Finally, there will be a simple little statement from the hospital staff, telling you how glad they are to welcome you to the hospital.

The expectant father could perhaps accept all of this, at least with a kind of stiff-upper-lippedness, were it not for the unfairness shown him. We do not refer, let the record show, to the fact that fathers wanting sons usually get the opposite, and vice versa; that is not completely the hospital's fault. What is unfair is the fact that many men are informed that they are parents long ahead of others who come to the hospital hours *before* them!

The point is not really to figure out a better way to have babies or take care of expectant fathers, however. Having a baby is a joyful time, a time about which we can laugh *after the event is over*. But we know that while the husband waits and the mother labors, it is truly an anxious time. Most people have waited, or one day will wait, in a hospital for a loved one. Hospitals deal with pain and often death.

The caricature of the expectant father is both a symbol of concern and a living testimony to our finitude. The mystery of birth and the mystery of death both demand courage and faith. Both happen to all persons, and when they occur, science with all its power and man with all his ingenuity are incapable of providing guarantees that birth *will* take place and death will *not*. So, those who care wait, and we laugh about their waiting to ease the human anxiety common to us all.

The Christian community can share in that waiting and take upon itself some of the anxiety of its members. The expectant father, the laboring mother, the person waiting out a crisis—these are able to wait alone if they know they are not alone. The love of God is most clearly shown through the love of people who care.

Prayer: *O Father, help us in the church to care for all who experience anxiety and loneliness. Keep us from ever assuming that because we are not afraid, there is no fear in the land. In the name of the One who gives us new life. Amen.*

On Becoming a Teen-ager

Between the innocence of childhood and the dignity of adulthood, there comes into being one of God's most complex creations—that unusual person called a teen-ager. Teen-agers come in assorted sizes, weights, and colors, but they all share a common creed: "To keep all adults in a state of anxiety, fluctuating between high hopes for the future of the world and complete despair for all living things."

Teen-agers are found everywhere—sprawling on, sitting cross-legged in the way, stretched out beside, or late getting to. Teachers fear them, parents can't understand them, ministers act silly trying to identify with them, and long-haired musical groups control their very lives.

When you are busy, a teen-ager dedicates himself to the playing of phonograph records, all of which make an adult feel old and tired because he can still remember when songs had words and music. When you want one to make a good impression, its brains turn to jelly and it may well demonstrate all the symptoms of African sleeping sickness. Or,

17

should it so choose, it may exude a charm which restores one's faith in God, man, and the reproductive process.

Teen-agers speak in tongues—not of men or angels but in tongues unlike any known to linguists or mystics the world around. Females of the species speak of "checking out a beauta-mus boy whose bod is utter coolness." Males utter such truths as "my retarded folks will stop my clock if I don't skate out for the homestead." Both sexes, when we're able to tell the difference, use such terms as "hairy deal," "hurtin'" and "checking out"—as in, "I had this big hairy deal going with this guy who's really hurtin', but I kept checking out Mr. Wonderful, waiting for my chance to move." * The only safe way to communicate with a teen-ager is to say "yeah" occasionally, "no" often, and nothing when asked for money.

Nobody but a teen-ager is so hard to get up in the morning or so difficult to get to bed at night. No other human being has his heart broken so often, or recovers so fast. Nobody else can talk so long on a telephone and say less than a teen-ager. Nobody else can find more excuses for not studying, or do a better job of reminding us we were the same way once.

Teen-agers are frustrating and flattering, discouraging and challenging, vague as midnight or forthright as a prophet. They can be subsidized but not analyzed. They hold no man or institution in awe, but their loyalties, once established, run deep and wide. They delight in testing us, trying our patience, confronting our ideals, and challenging our ideas. They are both our masters and our slaves, asking us for money and resenting our affluence.

* Translation: "I was on a date with an unattractive boy, but I am really more interested in another handsome boy."

We do well to accept them, better to trust them, and best of all to love them. They remind us of our own mistakes (and our forgotten dreams), and they strip away the sham of our lives. They long desperately for examples, for heroes, for leaders to follow, and they look to us and find us wanting. And this angers us, for they show us both what is right with the world and wrong with ourselves.

There is little doubt they could be better—much better—but there is even less doubt that the world would be worse (and much less interesting) without them. Between thirteen and nineteen a child disappears and an adult is born. Whether these birthdays are to be celebrated or mourned will depend on faith, hope, and love. Our faith in our own children will be sorely tested, for parents see in their children an extension of themselves, and, deep inside, we can remember the hidden fears and anxious doubts that plagued us at this time in our lives. Will they be able to break new ground and face old foes? Will they be stronger than we were, and, if so, can we accept their strength?

How much will our world let them realize their highest hopes? If we've taught them idealism, honor, and truth, dare we let them think such hopes can be realized? Dare we, though, let them see our own compromises?

Faith and hope will not be enough. The degree to which the love of parents and children for each other can be sustained in these crucial years is the heart of the matter. Faith and hope are essential, but love still makes the difference.

Prayer: O God who loves us all, help teen-agers to cut their emotional umbilical cords as painlessly as possi-

ble. Help them forgive us for our bad memories and us to forgive them for their rudeness and irreverence. Deliver us from too much analysis of ourselves as parents and our children as teen-agers. Help us to love well enough to overcome our problems, and stay especially near until our children are grown. In the name of Him who disturbed his elders. Amen

On Turning Thirty

Today's college student and somewhat older hangers-on face a truly traumatic crisis. Given our present world with its internal divisions, it is fair to say that we are in an era of war between the old and the young. Furthermore, the chronological lines have been drawn, and it has been made abundantly clear that the one dividing line which is irrevocable, which divides the younger generation from the older, and which causes today's revolutionary to acquire sweaty palms just thinking about it is the thirtieth birthday.

Consider the plight of the postgraduate or professor-activist or young minister who awakens to the fact that in a week or ten days he will become thirty years of age. Share with him the thoughts that must cross his mind as he contemplates that moment of truth.

Will he suddenly stop being the committed, relevant, one-of-the-gang person he has been since his undergraduate days and instantaneously metamorphose into an inane, irrelevant, carping old goat?

Will he change from a keen-minded, open-minded, fair-minded, piercing intellect into a fuzzy-thinking, shallow-thinking, backward-looking dullard, longing for the good old days that never were?

21

As he blows out those thirty terrible candles, will he suddenly stop believing in peace and love and brotherhood and
open dormitories? Will he, as his rhetoric has hinted, con-
struct an altar made entirely out of dollar bills, at which he
will pray fervently?

Dear God, will he find himself agreeing with everything
written in *U.S. News and World Report?* Will he, one day
soon, volunteer to drive a tank in the local Loyalty Day
Parade?

Will he, like those who have gone before him, roam the
campus of his beloved activist undergraduate days, pulling
apart kissing couples and forcing long-haired boys to cut
their hair and look like Pete Rose?

Most importantly, will he stop speaking the truth and
utter nothing but lies? Will he even, one day, in his very
depths, deliberately watch the Lawrence Welk show?

Such are the terrors of turning thirty, comparable probably only to those terrors we feel as we stare at the youth
of today from the other side of the generation gap. Why
can't they be as we were, nearly perfect in every way? We
studied hard and got ahead. We usually did what we were
told and did not ask why. We helped college fraternities enjoy their finest hours, and football rallies and pantie raids
were the social highlights of the season. We danced and
turned over cars and poured beer on each other's heads and
talked about "making it" with the girls. None of this business of peace marching or sit-ins or protests. And we were,
after all, neatly groomed.

The fact is, fellow Christian, that these times cry for reconciliation. The generations are glowering at each other,
attacking each other's stereotypes in a way that would make
the lies about mothers-in-law seem truthful. The division

affects the church, our colleges and universities, and most other institutions, and old and young seem older and younger to the other each day.

In a world full of problems and temptations, with wolves disguised as sheep and, in the minds of some, devils dressed in angels' robes, we cannot afford the luxury of verbal inquisitions. Whether we be Christian or pagan, in the church or outside, the need for reconciliation between the generations is as great as it has ever been in history. We are hurting each other badly, for we are striking at each other's most vulnerable parts—at pet ideas, long-standing beliefs, and personal self-images. Age thirty can be a Waterloo, but one where there can be neither winners or losers.

Reconciliation begins with self-examination. It begins with the hard, painful look at ourselves, our prejudices, and our own insecurities which we so often project on those whom we criticize. The young are no less guilty than the old, nor more so, and age thirty is as good a time as any to confess the oldest and most subtle sin of all—the sin of self-righteousness. For how can we be honest with others until we are honest with ourselves, and who can be honest with himself unless he levels with the One he calls God?

Prayer: O God, forgive our stubbornness. Forgive our unwillingness to listen to each other. Forgive our tendency to nit-pick, to despise others because their hair is too short, their sideburns are too long, or their words make us uneasy. Forgive us, but don't let us think that, once forgiven, we can continue to hate and call it the generation gap. In the name of the One who challenged all conformities and nonconformities. Amen.

On the Thirteenth Wedding Anniversary

Certain wedding anniversaries are so significant that society itself honors them. Among them, of course, is the 25th anniversary, at which time friends present congratulations and gifts of silver. Most couples who have reached this plateau are usually happy, too, as all their children are probably grown and away from home, and they are finally free to use the car themselves. At this stage, also, there are still a few places they want to go and sufficient adrenalin to get them started.

The Golden Wedding Anniversary also is honored by society, as well it should be, for it is to marriage what the two-mile run is to track: when you have made it that far, you know you've accomplished something even though you're too tired to appreciate it. On this occasion gifts of gold are to be presented, and all the children and grandchildren show up as living reminders of a couple's main achievements.

Heretofore neglected, however, has been the thirteenth wedding anniversary, an occasion which has its own significance as we meditate upon it. Statistics show, for instance, that the number of divorces radically decreases after thirteen years of married life. If you've made it this far, the odds are in your favor that you, too, will one day collect that silver loot and pose for pictures with all those grandchildren. The chances are that from this time on the thought of divorce will not cross your mind. Murder, yes, but not divorce!

This particular anniversary is significant too because thirteen is normally regarded as unlucky. As the statistics to which we referred indicate, however, this is not the case. Nevertheless, it is fair to say that by this time all illusions about marriage have been stripped away. The bridal wreath has long ago withered, and it is beginning to be difficult to remember who was an usher and who a groomsman in the wedding. The wedding dress has been folded away or perhaps even sold. The husband has come to accept the fact that her biscuits will always be inedible, and she no longer cares that her husband of thirteen years has legs like pipestems.

The love nest in the suburbs they rejoiced over in the third year of marriage now has a leaky roof, but by this time when they make their mortgage payments, more is directed toward the principal than toward the interest. Contrary to youthful opinion, the couple will probably still smooch a lot, but they seldom really get to enjoy a good necking session because one of their kids will be feeling rejection because his parents are not paying absolute attention to him.

Indeed, given the amazing way children have of interrupting romance or barging into bedrooms, it is surprising that anybody ever has more than one child. The fact that most couples married thirteen years do have more than one child is a tribute to *ingenuity*, locked doors, and weekend visits to Grandmother.

The high hopes, nay, dreams, of such couples have been set aside. The summerhome gives way to an extra bedroom, braces on teeth replace the trip to Hawaii, and it suddenly occurs to the breadwinner of the family that he no longer is experiencing as much "upward mobility," as the sociologists call it, as he did even two or three years ago. Wives accept the fact that their husbands are going to watch football on television by the hour (or day), and the husbands have learned to be *very* cheerful when emerging from in front of the set after a Sunday doubleheader.

As observed by college students and youthful romantics, this time of life and marriage is certainly not coveted and perhaps even anticipated with dismay. Secret vows are made "not to get so tied down" or to "keep romance alive" or to "take a trip to Europe while young enough to enjoy it," promises that are vaguely familiar to couples married for thirteen years because they once vowed such declarations themselves.

Youthful observers may be right, of course, and there exists always the real possibility that persons who have lived together as husband and wife for this many years will merely coexist and simply share what Thoreau called "lives of quiet desperation." Yet, what outsiders looking on may overlook is that a Christian marriage of this vintage understands the nature of love with a depth and insight that any couple with fewer anniversaries cannot have. They have come to know that love is more than an itchy feeling around the heart you cannot scratch, and many such couples look back on the early days of their marriage and laugh at their own feelings of love that they were sure, then, could never be more genuine.

The religious views and personal commitment to Christ of such persons have much to do with the joy of their marriage, but the maturity of their love is most clearly seen in the day-to-day quality of their relationship. At last they understand I Corinthians 13, where Paul talks about love as patience and kindness, about its not rejoicing in the wrong but in the right, about believing, hoping and enduring all things—even mortgages, disappointments, and skin blemishes. Such couples are in love, they have always been in love, and they know what it means to be blessed by God.

Prayer: Father, bless the years of married life that bring persons closer to you and to each other. Help men and women to see your hand in their marriages, that they may know you are with them through mortgage payments, payroll deductions, and even forgotten anniversaries. In the name of the One who blessed marriage at Cana. Amen.

On Turning Thirty-Five

Metabolism, as any good (or even mediocre) student of physiology and anatomy will tell you, consists of two parts: anabolism, building up; and catabolism, tearing down. During the springtime of our lives—say, between eighteen and twenty-five—anabolism exceeds catabolism. In other words, we build muscles, enjoy sexual vitality, and fairly glow with exuberance and health. Or at least we're supposed to, and certainly nature is on our side.

Between twenty-five and thirty-five, however, catabolism exceeds anabolism, and on birthday number thirty-five or thereabouts, we suddenly become conscious of the fact that the young, vibrant mare or stallion, as the case may be, is not what she or he used to be.

More specifically, what was once (at least in your mind's eye) a sleek, smoothly running machine now shows the signs of used-car-ness. Your skin is a little drier and a little thinner, and all those little blood vessels begin to show through; pink cheeks are yours no longer, and in fact you may look a bit purple. The veins in your legs have one-way valves in them which, at about this time, go limp and the vein bulges outward; that is, you have varicose veins and you look awful in swimming trunks.

Whereas once you needed a haircut every two weeks, you now are losing hair faster than you are growing it. The hair you do have is getting gray because the pigment in each carefully groomed blade is disintegrating and being replaced by air. The less than happy news, too, is that there is no effective treatment that is more pleasant than the problem.

Remember those milkshakes after the old ball game, the ones with double scoops of ice cream and flavored with butterscotch? They were loaded with cholesterol and other naughty components which collect in your blood vessel walls. As a result your calf muscles cramp, and a little bit of exercise makes you feel like a basket case in the senility ward of the old folks' home. You will have your midnight pizza, won't you, in your ongoing efforts to identify with your children, but now you can count on your stomach lining to pour out excessive acid in response to the anchovies and tomato sauce. By 2:00 A.M. you have gastritis. You also burp a lot.

You now burn only 2,600 calories a day, so you store the other 1,000 behind that ever-expanding belt, and your shape gradually assumes that of Santa Claus. Ho! Ho! Ho! Your prostate glands swell and block off the end of the bladder, and your nocturnal habits now include frequent visits to the bathroom. Ho! Ho! Your groin may be bulging, too, and as the muscles of the lower abdomen weaken and sag, your innards push them outward, and you've got yourself a hernia. Ho!

Hiding just beyond the horizon are gallstones, arthritis, farsightedness, bone spurs, flatfeet, and sagging jowls. The discs that cushion your vertebrae wear out at about thirty-five or thirty-six and pop. When this happens, it smarts a lot, although the pain may take your mind off your ulcer, which was acquired worrying about your loss of memory caused by the wearing out of your brain cells. Happy birthday, dear 35-year-old, happy birthday to you!

The morals, fellow sufferers, that can be drawn are legion. We need to be reminded to live temperate lives, that life is short, and that growing older cannot be avoided. We choose, however, to stress one other fact of God's creation of which we are reminded by our inescapable catabolism: we need to concern ourselves with relationships—love, mercy, sensitivity, concern—for they, truly, are the important verities of life. Unlike our liver or pancreas, and our joints, their qualities should increase, not diminish, with age. At least, it is not inevitable that they will fade away.

So, after thirty-five, mind, spirit, and soul abide, these three, and they are all greater than the body with its many infirmities. If we take this truth seriously, we can better understand what Jesus meant when he urged us to seek first his Kingdom. Unfortunately, there is little evidence that chronological age brings new Christian maturity. In fact, it may bring spiritual hardening of the arteries—Pharisaism. Age thirty-five may be the time when we notice we don't care as much as we should for the downtrodden, and we discover a heart problem unable to be cured by the doctor. We may even learn the truth that we don't have the truth, that we must continue to grow in wisdom and stature and, most importantly, in favor with God.

Prayer: Dear God, we thank you for our bodies, as ugly as they are and as feeble as they may become. Help us to use what strength we have to build relationships with others and with you. Spare us excessive worry over our health and inspire us to worry more about our neighbors who need our help. In the name of the Great Physician. Amen.

On Reaching Retirement

Once upon a time the aged were honored because of their years. To be old was a distinction. It was synonymous with wisdom and authority. Young people came to the old for advice and counsel, and older people felt a sense of achievement for having survived to a ripe old age. As the Old Testament suggests, a long life was a gift from God, even a sign of virtue, and "to be full of years" was far better than being young.

Today, however, such is not the case. Ours is a youth culture in which fashion, politics, art, music, literature, and restaurants are responsive to the young. Furthermore, the young and the not quite so young either ignore the old or treat them with open dislike. As Simon and Garfunkle say in one of their songs, "How terribly strange to be seventy." Anyone who has spent much time around college campuses notices the indifference with which alumni in general, and especially aged alumni, are often treated. Students think nothing of rolling semiclad on the grass, patrolling the hall-ways barefoot outside the room where a fiftieth anniversary tea is being held, and appearing their hippiest when the old people are around. Older alumni don't think much of it, either, and they feel about as welcome as King Farouk at a Bar Mitzvah when they visit anyplace where large numbers of youth gather. Young ministers don't like to "hold the hands of little old ladies," and the clergy and the doctors don't make house calls the way they used to do.

Thus, the goal of many people—to retire and enjoy life—has come to be a less desirable goal. For people with money, good health, careful plans, and lively interests, retirement can be a welcome time to do the things they always dreamed of doing. For many others, retirement means sitting on a park bench feeding pigeons or settling in a new retirement community to work at having fun via shuffleboard and cribbage. Those who want to work beyond retirement usually don't get an opportunity to do so, as mandatory retirement is the rule rather than the exception.

What's a grandmother to do? One thing she, or her male counterpart, can do is know the truth about aging. Recent studies of the aging have shown that the overwhelming majority of the aged can fend for themselves, and old people usually experience hypochondria only when their families criticize them unjustly or make them feel unwanted. In short, the sins of the children are visited upon their fathers when they treat them as senile, grouchy, old bags. Indeed, if the characteristics of senility are listed as being neurotic, negative, dissatisfied, socially inept, and unrealistic, college students may have more in common with the aged than anyone thought possible!

Sex researchers Masters and Johnson have found that men and women who enjoyed sex earlier in life can continue to enjoy it many years past sixty-five. Chances are many retired

people have discovered this on their own and have not found
it necessary to ask permission from social scientists to
manage their own sex lives. In fact, when we think about it,
it is absurd for youth to act as if they discovered sex, for
all ages have sexy people.

The point is that, as the Bible says, everything has its
season and all life moves toward death. Nothing has really
changed in that we seek fulfillment, joy, purpose, and meaning at every age. Retirement simply means that it is sought
in new ways, and thousands of persons have transformed
their years past sixty-five into golden ones. The incomparable
Grandma Moses can be the rule, rather than the exception,
and one octogenerian may have expressed this spirit by a
comment to his grandson. The youth, a college student,
wanted to know if his grandfather was ready to face death.
In reply, the old man said, "Yes, and I would like to be shot
by a jealous husband."

There is more truth than fiction in such an attitude, for its
humor directs us to a profound insight. The aged have the
responsibility to show the next generation how to face life's
ultimate concerns. Or, if you prefer a classic way of stating
it, perhaps the words of a Harvard psychologist will do:
"Any span of the [life] cycle lived without vigorous meaning, at the beginning, in the middle, or at the end, endangers
the sense of life and meaning of death in all whose life
stages are intertwined." In other words, if we are young
or old or in between, we accept each day as a gift. It is a
gift from God, and those who view their lives as such will
see retirement as a new opportunity to know God and serve
people in new ways. They may, in fact, find these days to be
so golden and rich that they will even be able to forgive the
society which shuns them.

Prayer: Oh God of all ages, if we are young, help us to know and relate to the aged. If we are old, help us to be understanding of the queer ways of the young, that all might see you better and do your will as long as our bodies allow us to do so. Help us rejoice in the fact that if we are not growing older, we are dead. In the name of Him who is ageless. Amen.

On Halloween

"When the frost is on the pumpkin and the fodder's in the shock," as James Whitcomb Riley once wrote, autumn is really here. If, however, one is not able to observe pumpkins growing and thinks fodder is simply Mudder's husband, there are other signs that the season has arrived.

For, wherever we live, whatever we do, it is impossible to avoid the celebration of Halloween. Come the end of October, every community will be descended upon by little creatures and their ghoulish friends. Children who otherwise are not allowed to cross the street roam in packs. Armed with great sacks, they work both sides of the street with the traditional ultimatum, "Trick or treat, smell my feet, give me something good to eat." Witches, goblins, bunny rabbits, ghosts, hobos, demons, skeletons, lions, tigers, and cowboys appear on every doorstep in such abundance that strict teetotalers have assumed they were suffering from the DTs, and more than one alcoholic has given up drinking altogether.

Whole communities organize for the event, adding extra police to direct traffic, establishing hours for the great shakedown to occur, and encouraging the citizenry not to put razor blades in the apples passed out to the kids. Local businesses feature Halloween specials, and the children usually collect enough sweets to upset their stomachs, destroy their appetites, and advance substantially the decay of their teeth.

Parents, as usual, get to share in the festivities too. They get to chaperone groups of goblins as they descend upon each house in turn. They get to deal with the child who inevitably will have to go to the bathroom and invariably will be dressed in a costume consisting of at least three layers of clothing. Parents also get to "help" carve faces on pumpkins, a chore which has its creative aspects, but includes as well the something-less-than-thrilling task of scooping out handfuls of pumpkin innards because the kids don't like that part of the project.

It's all good clean fun, however, and to be seriously critical of Halloween is unnecessary and probably grounds for deportation. Nevertheless, the celebration of Halloween as it takes place in the United States in the 1970s has an interesting history and raises some sobering questions for us. We note that two holidays immediately follow Halloween and, in fact, originally gave it birth. One is All Saint's Day, which takes place on November 1 and is observed in the Roman and Anglican traditions. It is a day upon which saints not otherwise mentioned by name in the calendar and those whose names are not known in the church militant are commemorated. The other holy day, which falls on November 2 each year, is All Soul's Day, an occasion observed with solemn services, usually including Requiem Masses. The day commemorates "holy souls" who have departed this life and are in the intermediate state awaiting their final end.

To most Christians, however, these occasions are virtually

unknown, and to learn that Halloween once had sacred and serious connections is a complete surprise. Yet, over the years an evolution has taken place in which an original intent—honoring the departed—has been transformed into a totally secular occasion. We have moved from Requiem Masses to masses of small children shouting "boo" at passers-by. The dominant theme as observed in our culture is more often expressed by a series of horror movies on TV than by a service commemorating Christian saints.

This evolution, in fact, may be the scariest part of Halloween. In spite of all the sermons about keeping Christmas Christian and not turning Easter into a secular style show, most Christians don't really fear that these days will one day lose their sacred roots. Halloween stands as a sobering example that it can happen.

Yet, there is a redemptive possibility present, too, which may remind us that God is still in charge of the world and not bound by any of our holidays, and certainly not our interpretations of them. God is surely in the joy and laughter of little children, and their squeals of delight and excitement are pleasing to him. There is the very real possibility, further-more, that a peculiarly modern use of Halloween may make it an occasion closer to the will of God than All Saint's Day has ever been. As children trick or treat for UNICEF, we may be seeing an important event occurring in front of our very eyes. We see children rising above greed to work for others. As they learn the meaning of what they are doing, hope can be felt again that a new generation may have more compassion for the world's hungry and poor than the old souls ever had.

It is difficult, perhaps impossible, to identify with cer-tainty which of the things we do and say and sponsor are of God and which are only of men; this is why Christianity is ultimately a religion of faith. Yet, in faith, we can affirm that God is Lord of the living and the dead, of Halloween and All Souls, of children with full stomachs and those who starve. If this strange occasion can remind us of this truth, it will be a holy day and not just a holiday. And one day we might even hear a child say, "Trick or treat, in the name of Christ."

Prayer: O God who is Lord of all, help us to separate substance from form in our holidays. Give us the vision to see you hard at work in the world and the sensitivity to discover you in unexpected places. In the name of Him who surprised his contemporaries as he surprises us still. Amen.

On a White
Christmas

Ever since Irving Berlin wrote "White Christmas," we have had a certain stereotype of the holiday which is the standard for what this occasion of occasions should be. In our minds' eye we envision gaily decorated Christmas trees, the sound of carols ringing through the air, the sight of snow-banked fields, the chatter of rosy-cheeked shoppers hurrying through the stores, and the familiar greeting of "Merry Christmas" on everybody's lips.

As Christmas approaches, we get warm and tingly inside as we think of the happy sight of our little families—of children and dogs gathered about the tree reading the Christmas story together. A lump rises in our throats as we dream of a white Christmas in which our days and nights are merry and bright.

The illusions of the Christmas season, however, never quite materialize. The lump in the throat is often replaced by a lump on the head from a shopper's flying elbow. The manger scene, once unpacked from its long hibernation, reveals itself to be missing one shepherd or to have a three-legged camel. Suddenly, it becomes the mangy scene. The family may indeed sit down to read the Christmas story together, only to hear at least one child (who will probably one day be an organizer for SDS) exclaim: "Let's open the presents right now!" So much for the lovely domestic scene when that happens.

Some of us would very much like to hear the sound of Christmas carols ringing through the air, but about all we ever get to hear, it seems, are the renditions having to do with some poor child who has lost his two front incisors or that lovely ballad poetically entitled "Jingle Bell Rock." Snow, of course, we may get, but it loses some of its charm when mingled with the mud of Twelfth Street where they're putting in a new gas line and digging ditches all over the place. Our days often end up being muddy and white.

Feverishly, we write those cards and lick those stamps until our fingers cramp and our mouths taste like glue. Stores raise their prices, and advertisers bombard us with the message that all will be lost if we don't immediately spend money we haven't got to buy things that will probably be lost in the mail to pay back somebody who unexpectedly gave us a gift we didn't want last year. As our children become monsters before our very eyes, and as we cough and sneeze from the cold we caught while caroling in the dirty old snow, perhaps those of us with little faith may be heard to utter the timid blasphemy: "Somehow it just doesn't seem like Christmas!"

And so it doesn't. Seldom does reality measure up to the artificial and sentimental vision of Christmas which Hollywood, Hallmark cards, the Chamber of Commerce, and our own bad memories create for us. If we are honest, in fact, we must admit that Christmas is something of a disappointment. It just doesn't measure up to what Bing Crosby and the Goodyear Christmas record promised.

So much the better! The heart of Christmas is not an illusion but reality. Jesus was not born during the time of Old King Cole but when Herod, a cruel and violent man, was king. Christ came to remind us that we have a continuous responsibility to the poor, the lonely, the lost, the searching, the miserable, and the self-satisfied.

If the only message of Christmas were to enjoy oneself, to be gay, or to be merry and bright, the season would be a complete disaster. One can test this fact by simply observing any person who has lost a loved one on or near Christmas. The holiday, far from being a time of happiness, immediately becomes the saddest time of the year. Thank God we have more to say to such persons than "please be merry and bright." Thank God, too, that we can know that God still is in charge of the universe in spite of personal experiences of sorrow. "Joy to the World" is not the same as "White Christmas," for joy and hope are kindred spirits, and snow disappears as the seasons change.

Thus, when our children act naturally, this seldom means that they sit silent, docile, and obedient just because it's Christmas. Why should this season be without frustrations and disappointments? After all, such circumstances as these are the very ones Christ came to heal. The real Christmas belongs in our kind of world, for we are the kind of people who need its message—the message that God is with us, Emmanuel has come, and the hope for peace is still alive, in spite of the way things are.

Prayer: *O God of Christmas, help us not to confuse the stuff of Christmas with the truth of Christmas. Help us not to anticipate an illusion when you have given us reality. Help us to experience happiness because we know that the Joy of the world has come. In the name of the One for whom there was no room in the inn. Amen.*

On the Night Before Christmas

Contrary to the well-known poem, on the night before Christmas considerable creaturely activity is stirring. True, children are asleep, elderly persons are asleep, and most mice are asleep. However, fathers and mothers of small children are not asleep; they are awake trying to put together into recognizable wholes toys which are supposed to bring squeals of delight from children at 5 A.M. (three hours later).

What most consumers, Christian or pagan, annually forget is that one does not buy toys or wagons or tricycles or supersonic things as gifts. One only buys a box in which are contained the *component parts*, more or less, of the item he thought he was buying.

In the advertisements, the catalogs, and the store windows, that which we wish to buy (or, at least, are psychologically manipulated into buying) is there to behold—shiny, bright, luxuriously displayed, and *totally assembled*. However, that which we end up buying is usually a collection of parts, nuts, bolts, screws, and springs, a carefully calculated percentage of which are too small for holes or too large for slots where they supposedly belong.

The box will come equipped with a complete set of directions so simple that any Ph.D. from the Massachusetts Institute of Technology could follow them in a year—if he had a crew of men to help and a psychiatrist standing by. In short, for those gifted few who, as the saying goes, are "handy about the house," putting things together under the pressure of Christmas expectations is less than a traumatic experience. To many of us, however, who cannot hang pictures straight or dismantle an electric razor for cleaning, the entire situation breeds inferiority feelings that make Charlie Brown seem like an egomaniac.

Thus, our children feel neglected because they have a wagon which has one wheel that refuses to turn. We broil our hamburgers on a grill so wobbly that burning coals roll from side to side. Our sons end up playing with dolls because the jungle gym we purchased is lopsided, undoubtedly due to the fact that we used a hammer to pound the "short uprights" over the "long uprights" when, according to the directions, one was to "slip easily over the other"!

Our daughters, who are supposed to play happily by the hour with their new toy kitchen, experience considerable parental rejection as they ask their mother to fix again and again and again the faucet on the toy sink so water will flow out and not down onto the rug. Mother, whose new blender doesn't work because a part is missing, demonstrates her hostility by fixing bologna sandwiches for lunch—without pickles. Merry Christmas to all, and to all, an Excedrin headache!

Even when we get the rail track put together on which the plastic cars are supposed to zoom at phenomenal speeds, we discover that such equipment never includes batteries, even though batteries are what enable the cars to run. Furthermore, practically no stores in the world are open on Christmas that sell batteries, and so fathers and sons spend much of the day nursing wounds and disappointment. If the child is eight or older, he doubts his father's sincerity, and, if younger, the kid regards Santa as an overweight fink.

Let us face it, fellow consumers, ours is a do-it-yourself age whether we can do it ourselves or not. Chances are, this is a situation which is not going to change, and we can expect the night before Christmas to be spent in putting things together and quite possibly hating Christmas, resenting children, and despising ourselves. It just may not seem like Christmas.

The problem, of course, lies within us. Just as Christmas joy is not really dependent upon tricycles, wagons, toy kitchens, and charcoal grills, neither can we blame unhappiness on the fact that things don't go right. Of course things don't go right! Whatever fiendish plots are abroad in the land to frustrate and provoke us, the truth is that they will all fail if we are able to laugh at life and its foibles. The man who lets a missing bolt ruin Christmas has a spiritual problem, and the children whose psyches are warped because their new wagon came prebroken will simply have to rise above their disappointment in not getting to break it themselves. After all, the Lord has come to heal the broken-hearted and, with this in mind, we can know that God, not anarchy, still rules the world.

Prayer: O God, who rules the universe, forgive our poor planning and human awkwardness; both that which those who manufacture things exhibit and that which we show the night before Christmas. Help us to laugh at ourselves when we are foolish, which is often. In the name of Him whose birth we honor. Amen.

On New Year's Eve

To thousands of Americans, New Year's Eve is the favorite holiday. Thanksgiving, Christmas, and Easter all have religious connotations, and even though society has virtually transformed them into folk festivals, vague guilt feelings often inhibit some of the celebrants on those holy days. At least, some gesture of giving thanks is expected on Thanksgiving, and the orgy of gift-giving or clothes-buying that overshadows Christmas and Easter do not escape public criticism.

Not so with New Year's Eve. New Year's Eve is the hedonist's holiday. It is the time to get "smashed," have a party, kiss other people's wives, and release inhibitions. Some churches attempt to have Watch Night programs for their youth, but these are sparsely attended because so many of the young people are baby-sitting for the multitudes who are giving or going to parties.

One interesting way to spend New Year's Eve in large cities is to go down to the heart of the city and stand with other people, by the hundreds, and shout "Happy New

Year" at 12:00 midnight. This is fun, if you relish getting elbows poked in your ribs and if you derive enjoyment from bruised toes and horns blasting in your ears. In fact, rumor has it that the Time Square midnight jamboree is really sponsored as a joint effort of the liquor industry and the Pickpocket Association of New York.

Another popular way of spending the evening is to go to a nightclub. In such a setting sober individuals are suspected of criminal tendencies. If you refuse to wear a paper hat or shout, you are immediately branded as a square who probably only dances with his wife. The most serious danger on such occasions is that you might double-Scotch yourself into telling acquaintances what you think of them. One and all seem dedicated to the idea that creating a hangover indicates supreme joy.

New Year's Eve is the time when otherwise dignified persons tell old and dirty jokes, when many of those dancing to Guy Lombardo's music lend credence to the TV commercial that girdles are, indeed, much too tight, and many others seem to be working harder at having fun than they ever do at earning a living. Walter Winchell, not a preacher by any means, sounded like one as he described the scene in one of his columns: "Nightclubs were generally dominated by a desperate gaiety. They lured those who fill vacant hours with nothing and found some consolation in sharing their emptiness. No matter how many zeros you added—the final total was always zero."

True, not all celebrate the coming of a new year in such a fashion, but millions do. The desperate gaiety of which Winchell speaks is a sign of the times and probably the most persuasive argument against hedonism there is. The search for happiness goes on and on, but experience confirms what the gospel has said all along: one does not find life by eating, drinking, and chasing Mary; one finds his life by losing it.

Our society says that happiness is being with the "right" people and making sure the wrong people don't get in. The spirit of the New Testament suggests that happiness is being with people you don't have to apologize to for your behavior of the night before.

Our society says that happiness is hanging one on on New Year's Eve. A different philosophy of life says that happiness is waking up on New Year's Day without a hangover and watching the Rose parade while eating popcorn instead of aspirins.

Madison Avenue tell us that happiness for our children is new toys which they are to wind up and break. The good news is that most children would rather have a turtle from the dime store; happiness is not only a warm puppy—it is also a damp turtle.

New Year's Eve in a nightclub seems to show that a lot of men and women are not completely satisfied with the company of their own spouses. Real happiness is available to the person who can come home to the one to whom he is married with a clear conscience.

We all want happiness, and the God who revealed himself in Jesus Christ wants us to have it, too. Yet his children at play on New Year's Eve demonstrate a timeless truth: happiness comes when we look in the right places and in the right ways. Otherwise, as sure as a hangover follows getting tight, we'll be disappointed, and we will find only "kicks" but never joy.

Prayer: O God of the ages, forgive us for being spoilsports and party poopers, but forgive us also for going along with the silliness of our society and the immorality that seems fashionable. Help us to do your will, for we know we can then find joy without seeking it and happiness while sober. In the name of Him by whom we reckon time. Amen.

On Easter Happiness

Let us reflect together upon the meaning of Easter Sunday. Countless meditations on this theme have already been written, of course, practically all of which are more profound than this one and to which we commend your attention. Easter, after all, is not an occasion at which any Christian can poke fun, for it continues to be the central mystery of the church, not to be taken lightly.

Easter Sunday as observed by humble servants, however —who, by the way, have every reason to be humble—is a different matter. The human personality has shown itself capable of reducing any occasion, no matter how significant, to one of trivia or even buffoonery. Our society has transformed Easter, for example, into a style show. It is significant that Irving Berlin, a Jew, captured the mood of the occasion for many Americans in his famous song, "The Easter Parade." Only on Easter Sunday do restaurants advertise with the words, "after church, eat at Joe's," the assumption being that such attendance is a onetime fact. Or we transform Easter into a rite of spring and vaguely identify the

Resurrection with the rebirth of the shrubs and the emergence of the crocus flowers. Our provincialism is exposed, however, when we recall that Easter celebrated in the southern hemisphere is synonymous with the coming of winter, for it occurs in the autumn there. Our naïveté is uncovered when we remember that countless Christians cannot afford new clothes at all, and the only Easter parade they know is waiting in line at the township trustee's office.

Still, Easter is not a morbid time, and perhaps we do well to expose our churchgoing foibles by poking fun at them, rather than by dwelling on the sins of our society. We invite you to test this statement by examining the following "inner" thoughts of certain persons on Easter Sunday, seeing how many of them have been yours or, perchance, attributed to others.

On the left side of the page are several statements of "Easter happiness" and on the right is a list of persons who might well have authored them. Try to match them.

1. Easter happiness is getting all dressed up, neat and clean, and not getting the chocolate rabbits on the new clothes.

2. Easter happiness is being able to look at a ridiculous hat and not laugh in someone's face.

3. Easter happiness is the preacher not giv-

(a) A once-a-year attender

(b) Any small child, age six or younger

(c) A minister who spent twelve hours in preparing his Easter sermon

(d) Almost any man with normal eyesight

(e) One of the few wives who did not get a new dress this year

ing the people the
dickens for coming
only once a year.
4. Easter happiness is
the annual 6 A.M.
breakfast without
cold eggs and burnt
toast.
5. Easter happiness is
a congregation full
of babies and small
children, without
any crying.
6. Easter happiness is
having someone tell
you how nice you
look, when your
dress is two years
old.

(f) The youth group
sponsors

Thoughts such as these have been, and will be, thought again at Easter time. As with other Christian holidays, our thoughts do not always—or even primarily—center on the life and resurrection of Jesus. This is only human, of course, but the ongoing responsibility of the Christian is to be *in Christ*, not simply the "natural" man, not "only human."

Thus, we do well to consider what might be a more appropriate definition of Easter happiness. Try this for size: Easter happiness is a change of heart, a new dedication, a new understanding of the gospel, or a new awareness of opportunity to witness to the reality of the living Christ in our lives.

Prayer: O God, help us to find the Living Christ in the midst of the fantasy, frustration, and fashion we now call Easter. Forgive us for acting as if the Resurrection has not occurred. Free us from our preoccupations so that Easter happiness can be for us a synonym for Christian joy.

In the name of Him who is the resurrection and the life. Amen.

On Mother's Day

For years only kind words have been reserved for mothers. Ever since the florists initiated Mother's Day, poems, prayers, and prose have been dedicated to Mom, her apple pie, and her aprons. The experience of most of us supports such feelings of sentiment, for few of you who read this book of meditations probably would be interested in religion at all were it not for the influence of your early childhood when Mother indeed was queen.

This is not so clear today. Women's Liberation, albeit with high motives, has caused some of our mothers to wonder if, in fact, they are victims of male chauvinism. Furthermore, with the current stress on the population explosion, if a mother has more than two children, she is regarded in many quarters as somewhat un-American, or at least unfit for membership in the League of Women Voters. This, plus the normal confusions the sociologists cause as they discuss the "roles" of the modern woman, understandably causes the conscientious, independent, idealistic woman to ask the deepest of all philosophic questions, "What's a mother to do?"

Before Women's Liberation, mother could live a perfectly contented enslaved life. She could prepare meals, keep the house neat, care for her children, and even iron her sheets if she so chose. She probably wouldn't talk much in public about her sex life, but the fact that she was a mother was evidence that she had one. Secretly she knew that the weaker sex was really the stronger sex because of the weakness of the stronger sex for the weaker sex.

Now, obviously, she doesn't know how to behave toward her husband or how to raise her daughters. If her husband has pet names for her, she may feel the necessity of being offended. To be called—even affectionately—"Cookie," "Gumdrop," "Sugar," or "Honey" is a male paternalistic device that treats women as things to be devoured. Beware of the man who refers to his wife as "Kitten," as this is a sexist plot to keep women in a weak and subservient role! So are girdles, hairspray, cosmetics, and the assumption of the last name of her husband.

Should mothers let their daughters play with dolls? Should they teach their sons how to cook and sew? Should they volunteer for the draft, and should a Mothers' Union be formed that will strip away arrogance from those sexual supremists—their husbands? Mother's Day this year could be the beginning of the end for the subservience of women and ring out a death toll for the gooey sentimentality long associated with the day!

Probably this won't happen. It won't happen not because women already have all their rights and freedom, for they don't. It won't happen because millions of women, thank God, see the business of child rearing as a Christian vocation. Whether or not the ability to train up a child in the way he should go is inherent or learned is a matter for social scientists to debate. Whether men, if stuck at home with all those diapers, dishes, skinned knees, and scattered toys, could do as effective a job in bringing order out of chaos and growth out of bedlam remains to be seen. Yet, the fact also stands that many women achieve such goals, and they perform their vocations very well. The woman, in short, who sees her role of mother as vocation may well be able to find the fulfillment she deserves, even if she postpones other interests until a later time.

From a man's point of view, too, we may revere our mothers for reasons that have nothing to do with the psychological desire to relegate women to the roles that show weakness and softness. In fact, we revere them because most of us know how rugged and tough some of our mothers (and some of our wives) really are. This writer's mother, who is about five feet two inches tall and delicate as a rose petal, has worked many sixteen-hour days, not only at home, but side by side with her husband in the family business. She has made hardheaded business decisions, driven, on a few occasions, a gasoline truck up and down southern Indiana hills, and proven herself an intellectual equal to her husband and most other men. Yet her sons honor her as a *mother,* not as a rugged individualist or business woman, and she, too, regards this role as her most significant one.

In short, motherhood ought not to be regarded as an imposed role or second-class citizenship. Downgrading it, in the minds of either men or women, is wrong because it is a vocation, not a job. It is vital to the lives of future as well as present generations. The biological facts which cause women to become mothers may have something to do with the vocation of motherhood, but they are secondary to the qualities of patience, love, and forgiveness which allow women to be persons and cause men, especially in their role as sons, to honor their mothers this year, or any other year.

Prayer: *Oh God, help us to treat each other as persons, not things. Help us to see our vocations, whatever they are. We thank you for the women of the world who have shown us what motherhood should be. In the name of Him who honored his mother at Calvary. Amen.*

On Wedding Gifts

Mental illness strikes every sixty seconds in the United States, but if the temporary insanity that afflicts the buyers of wedding presents is included, the frequency ratio would surely be higher. Consider the situation of the young bride and groom, surrounded by dozens of gifts, a significant percentage of which have been given by distant relatives or parental business partners who are total strangers to them. Probably it is late August, and the groom is dressed in flannel pants which itch, a starched collar which cuts into his neck like a hangman's noose, and shoes which pinch his feet. Consider, too, that he has been standing in a reception line for an hour greeting people who keep kissing his wife who, just a few minutes before, had promised to be faithful forever.

Then, perhaps, shortly thereafter he and his bride will be expected to open gifts, identify the persons who gave them, and then emit squeals of joy as evidence of ecstasy and sincere appreciation. This is often the moment of truth for the young couple, for some of the gifts over which they are expected to be ecstatic are a mystery beyond human comprehension.

What does the young groom say in that split second after having just opened "something" made of colored cut glass which has a neck a little like a bottle, the base of a jug, wings like an angel, and no possible function? Is it an objet d'art or did the junk man make a mistake and *leave* some this month instead of hauling it way? Consider, too, the fact that people who present such gifts are usually wealthy aunts who tempt whole families with the hint that they may be "remembered" in their wills.

Following are some suggestions to help such grooms and brides with this kind of situation, perhaps the most serious threat to their marriage until their children are born. Hopefully, these suggestions will enable the couple to do two seemingly contradictory things—both express their real feelings and still say something aloud that will not cause them to be written out of the will.

Suggestions	Translation
"Auntie, dear where did you ever find one like this?"	"I'd like to know in order to return it for something useful."
"Well, well, well—what do we have here?"	"What in the name of little green apples is this thing?"
"Auntie, darling, you really shouldn't have done so much."	"You shouldn't have done this to a dog."
"I'm overwhelmed. I just don't know what to say."	"I never swear when there are children present."

"Auntie, what a fun gift!"   "I think I'm getting hys-
                                        terical!"

In such devious ways as these, a young couple may survive
the first day of their wedded life (no mean achievement),
although we hope they'll be more honest with each other
than with their wealthy aunts. A more serious problem,
however, implied in the above essay is seen in what the
wedding ceremony has become. Weddings, even church weddings—*especially* church (translation, "big, expensive")—
weddings often seem less like a sacrament and more like an
extravaganza. They fairly breathe status-seeking, snobbish-
ness, and phoniness toward aunts. That which can and
should be one of the few genuinely holy and sacred occasions in the life of human beings frequently is an exercise
in keeping up with the Joneses, who are keeping up with the
Smiths, who are keeping up a good front till bankruptcy they
and their money doth part.

Beginning marriage with simplicity and openness—both
toward each other and toward those whose blessing is sought
—will honor both God and man. We ought to be encouraged
that many young couples are now seeking simpler weddings
for themselves, stressing honesty and integrity in their vows
and authenticity in the way they choose to begin their
married lives.

Herein, then, is the lesson. If ever there were a time for
sincerity, not phoniness; for beauty, not gauche display; for
joy, not silliness; and for communion with God, not a
thoughtless invocation of his name—it is when a man and a
woman seek God's blessing as they enter the holiest of all
human contracts.

Prayer: Father of us all, help us see the difference between ceremonies and sacraments. Help us by our example as well as by our words, bless the lives of those who marry in your name. In the name of Him who blessed the wedding at Cana. Amen.

On Visiting the
Beach

Summertime, when the living is easy, is the time when Americans by the score participate in that great exercise in hedonism, the vacation at the beach. Baseball is often called the national sport, but any person with one eye not blinded by the sun can see that the game played by more people than any other during the summer months is sunbathing.

The main field of play for this game is anywhere out of the shade. The beach, of course, is the favorite place, although in recent years participants have chosen to compete wherever they could do so without being arrested—and a few places where they were. As in churches, all ages and sexes can participate, but usually women show up the best.

The object of the sport is very simple. It is to see who can become the most nearly broiled, baked, burned, and browned without losing his sanity. Given the several levels of rationality among people, this puts some at a distinct disadvantage. For the most part, however, participants bare up well.

The game is primarily a spectator sport, a fact of which

female competitors seem more than a little conscious. Most of them wear what are usually called bathing suits, although many women never go near the water while wearing them. Given their freshly created coiffures and the high cost of the suntan lotion with which they oil their bodies, this is probably sensible.

Men at the beach (let us be honest) stare at the girls. In fact, part of the game is to see who can be the one stared at the most the longest. Thus, some girls wear suits which cause one to wonder whether they are inside getting out or outside getting in. Many girls wear just enough to keep from getting tanned where they should be for wearing so little.

The male of the species is not only a spectator, however. The aged and infirm male who has retired from competition sits on the sidelines behind his forty-inch waistline, peeking from behind sunglasses at the slim girls in their tiny suits. However, others, slightly younger, try to compete by strolling casually along the beach as if they were looking for clams, all the while holding their breath and pulling their stomachs in until they look more than a little deformed. Seldom do such persons win many followers.

The young bucks, however, compete intensely with their female counterparts as often as possible. These young men lift things, such as surfboards, beach balls, or girls. Such items may not need lifting, but the process puts on display muscles, tendons, and ligaments in a way that is calculated to bring sighs from nearly exposed hearts of the young girls and jealous snorts from the over-thirty-five crowd.

Indeed, there are some rare sights to behold, although most are medium or well-done. The point, which could easily be missed, is that sunbathing in America is frequently the manifestation of hedonism. Thousands of girls spend hundreds of hours at beaches and swimming pools doing little else than acquiring tans, combing hair, and comparing bodies. An equal number of older Americans migrate to warm climates, partly to relax, but to a considerable degree to show off their tans (status symbols) when they return. The emphasis on the body and the way it looks is a striking mark of our culture. Tanned girls in bathing suits sell soap, automobiles, hair lotion, and many other products. We are a nation preoccupied with the body, certainly to a far greater degree than the soul or spirit.

So what is wrong with this? Maybe not much, as this writer must confess that he, too, is both victim as well as critic of this phenomenon. Yet, when so much of our economy, so many of our values, and so great an expenditure of our time depend upon how people look while nearly naked, the question deserves to be asked. Worrying about our appearance, whether it be our suntans or the firmness of our figures, is to be concerned about externals rather than realities. It is ironic, in fact, to learn that human skin, when tanned by the sun year in and year out, has serious damage done to it. The "healthy, tanned look" is not really very healthy after all. A day at the beach should be a break from routine, a vacation from work, or an unwinding of tensions. When it becomes a way of life, the soft belly of our society is exposed and our moral flabbiness revealed.

Prayer: O God, who made the sun and sky, help us to worship you and not your creations. Help us to love people as whole persons—body, mind, and spirit. Help our love for others to be more than skin deep. In the name of the Word who became flesh. Amen.

On Taking Long Motor Trips with Children

Why aren't vacations more fun for more people? While some families have discovered ways to relax and enjoy each other's company on trips, many persons return from their vacations needing a vacation. Even a casual observer can notice signs of fun-less-ness at almost any tourist site along the way—if he looks about him. Surely, for example, there are more crying children per square foot in souvenir shops than there are in most nursery schools across America. A vacation often brings out in children a classic symptom of humanity which has been observed since Adam became the first victim of Women's Liberation: *greed*. A child in a souvenir shop on vacation quickly becomes convinced that his entire life will be ruined if he does not buy a plastic rocket with "welcome to Colorado" stenciled on its side and "made in Hong Kong" imprinted on its bottom.

Thus, he cries or stamps his feet or both, and the father who has driven eight hundred miles to get to this spot either will give in to the embarrassment of the situation and bribe the kid to shut him up, or yield to his own fatigue and frustration by screaming at and beating the product of his planned parenthood until the one with the most stamina and strength bullies the other into compliance. However, as in nuclear war, there are no victors, and the blasphemous thought may occur to both parent and child, "I wish we hadn't left home!"

Mealtimes, too, represent another high point in vacation low points. These occasions have all the ingredients for disaster from the outset, as the combination of excitement, the range of choices a menu offers, the lack of appetite resulting from snacking in the car, and the inevitable fact of constipation make the concept of gracious dining irrelevant. The child wonders why he must eat vegetables on vacation; his mother wonders how long her family can live on butterscotch sundaes and foot-long hot dogs; and her husband sits incommunicado, recalling his bachelor days or contemplating divorce. The restaurant staff, of course, is busy waiting on everybody else while your family *busily* waits. The experienced traveler doesn't mind waiting because the food is usually poor when it arrives, but children are not experienced travelers and the family on vacation at mealtime can become the family in crisis.

Magazines and other journals give us helpful hints as to how to make vacations more fun. They provide us with games to play in the car; for example, "count all the red cars you see." We are instructed to carry a jug of ice water at all times and make frequent rest stops. Hotels and motels make it easy for us to plan ahead by calling *free* one number through which we can make reservations for any place in the world, except possibly the city where we want to stay the next night.

All such advice is helpful and useful. However, it is fair to point out that there are some basic realities of life that must be faced before vacations will be fun or restful. Families that don't know how to be patient with one another won't suddenly learn while traveling across Kansas in August with the temperature at 110° Fahrenheit. Indeed, they'll probably get as hot as the weather. Children who are not confronted at home with the importance of values and the sinfulness of greed will only be tempted to a great degree by the hucksters of shiny junk, any of which could be bought at Woolworth's in your hometown.

In short, the basic Christian virtues of love, patience, forbearance, forgiveness, and kindness will undergird a family on vacation or at home. Without them, life will always be vaguely unsatisfactory, and with them adults and children will discover happiness wherever they are. The Christian faith, if real, will affect our style of life, and we will be able to appreciate Pike's Peak even on a cloudy day, and we may even rise above the plastic temptations which speak to our greed and weakness. We may even come to enjoy both the scenery and, through the grace of God, each other.

Prayer: O God who travels with us wherever we go, give us strength to resist cheap souvenirs and meaningless junk that corrupt our children and compromise our values. Quicken the steps of the waitresses in the restaurants, but if they are as tired from a hard day of working as we are from sight-seeing, give us the ability to smile and the grace to calm our children, that the tip we leave might be evidence of genuine appreciation. In the name of Him who traveled the dusty roads and still found peace. Amen.

On Going Camping

Most of us have the urge to get away from it all. Beneath our blue serge suits and paisley prints beats the heart of a wanderlust, and we long for the call of the wild—away from traffic, air pollution, the boss, the neighborhood influences that despoil our children, and (may we be forgiven!) even church.

Indeed, many Americans think of themselves as the last of the rugged individualists. Perhaps overcome by the nostalgic memories of Boy Scout days or a vague recollection of Thoreau's experiences at Walden Pond, we resolve to return to nature. Inspired by hopes of renewing our relationship with our children and warmed inwardly by the cozy thought of snuggling with our spouses in double sleeping bags, we plan a camping trip.

It is shortly thereafter when the realities of our situation hit us. We discover that we are not so unique after all and that a number of other hardy souls share our self-image, our dislike of air pollution, and our memories of Boy Scout days. More precisely, according to a recent issue of *The Campfire Chatter*, there are more than forty million family campers, and the number is growing at the rate of 15 percent a year. In New York State, for example, the demand for camping space is rising far faster than the supply, and between 1965 and 1970 about ninety thousand persons showed up at New York State campgrounds and had to be turned away because there was no room for them.

This means, in other words, that those who seek to get away from it all are getting in the way of those others who are seeking to get away from it all. It also means that camping enthusiasts now are being jammed for a weekend into 40-foot spaces lined up geometrically in neat patterns, with each concrete campsite equidistant from metal signs telling us not to cut firewood. In short, campgrounds are rapidly coming to be like a grocery store parking lot with outside toilets and only slightly less asphalt. Even the nature trails are as well marked as an interstate system, and there soon may be more bird watchers than birds along the paths.

It is still possible to get away from it all without tripping over each other, and many hardy souls are too proud (or too poor) to buy a truck camper which includes, as advertised, "a four-burner range with eye-level oven, 20,000 BTU forced air heater, six-cubic-foot refrigerator, and full fiberglass bathroom with molded-in floor, dinette, and color coordinated upholstery, draperies, and carpeting." This type of camping is, in the minds of some pioneer types, not a case of getting away from it all but taking it all away with you.

Such "true" descendants of the hardy pioneers will choose primitive camp grounds and isolated areas of wilderness, thereby demonstrating their authenticity as nature lovers by sleeping on the ground, cooking over an open fire, and depending upon maintenance-free, white polyethylene "Porta Potties" as their comfort stations. This, say the purists, is where man can truly get close to God and nature, where the air is clean and the water cold.

So it is. So it is also the place where you can get close to insects and many friendly varieties of bugs, as most un-inhabited places are usually inhabited by giant mosquitoes, black flies, and red ants. Cooking over an open fire is an exhilarating experience for men and children, although "vacationing" housewives have found it less enjoyable since they are usually the ones who do the cooking. Sleeping on the ground is fun, especially if you get up a few times in the night to rest.

Why do so many endure either the frustrations of portable civilization or the inconveniences of wilderness in the face of such realities? Not only is it, as we suggested above, an effort to satisfy our urges to return to nature once again, but there may be even a more fundamental need seeking fulfillment. A report for the United States Forest Service in 1968 gives us a clue. Based on a survey of 1,348 persons who had visited wilderness areas of Washington and Oregon, the report concluded that the "wildernist" rejoices in the "simplified role-playing and reduced status-seeking of the experience."

In other words, fellow campers, you and I are feeling a vague dissatisfaction with the daily lives that organized society forces upon us. We are tired of being an IBM card or a pin in somebody's organizational chart. Perhaps we're fed up with the phoniness of our society, both that which we see in others and that which corrupts our own souls. So we long not just to get away but to seek and find meaning and fulfillment for our existence.

Going camping, if it suits our taste, may help, but it may also help to remember that "the kingdom of God is within us." Now, as in the time of Jesus, we still must find peace for our souls and confront the frustrations of our lives at home or in a tent in Yellowstone National Park. The good news is that the source of help is available wherever we go, and this truth can enable us to endure modern society at its worst or primitive camping at its best.

Prayer: O God of the wilderness, help us to escape briefly the pressures of our lives that the living of them might be richer. Help us to see your hand in our sometimes silly efforts to handle our problems by escaping from them. Forgive us if we attempt to escape from, rather than face, our insecurities and help us find our rest in you. In the name of Him who spent forty days in the wilderness. Amen.

On Coffee Breaks

At approximately ten o'clock on any weekday morning, many millions of workers from California to New York will suddenly drop their tools on workbenches, abandon type-writers in mid-sentence, and leave bosses, telephones, and participles dangling in order to join their fellows in that great democratic rite known as the coffee break.

So widespread is this practice—according to statisticians who keep records of such goings on—that Americans will literally drink enough of the black liquid to float a large battleship through the St. Lawrence Seaway. The statisticians also reveal that it will take the entire day's output of 120,960 contented cows, munching grass at top speed, just to supply all those people with enough milk and cream for the ten-minute coffee stampede.

At least one fourth of all labor contracts now contain a Kaffeeklatsch guarantee, and in those firms which permit two caffein furloughs per day, sixteen full days per year of coffee-drinking (with pay) are used up.

The customer, visitor, or traveling salesman who should

happen to arrive during this sacred period has learned to accept as irrevocable the absence of all human personnel, with the possible exception of the company president who is trying to "set the pace" for his employees. Many bosses, knee-deep in paper cups, wooden spoons, and lumps of sugar, have taken surveys to find out if such regular breaks are really necessary to the health and well-being of the staff. No hard evidence has ever been secured, however, as few questionnaires were ever returned due to the fact all the employees were out on a coffee break!

The coffee break as an excuse for absence or being away from the old desk has supplanted other traditional and time-worn reasons such as stomach pains, hairdresser appointments, turning the oven down, and death in the family. Indeed, so universally accepted is the coffee break that its possibilities and potential for good boggle the mind. Armies could stop fighting each other long enough to share coffee, and if the break were extended as long as many are in a typical American business, peace could come to the world. Demonstrators at universities could take over the coffee shop instead of the president's office, and students and administrators might finally experience dialogue together. Estranged husbands and wives could come together over coffee, although refusal to meet even then would clearly be "grounds" for divorce.

Hidden deep beneath the humor and meaningful statistics of the above paragraphs, there is a lesson to be taken seriously. Our lives are more hectic than they used to be in the "good old days" (from the employer's perspective) before coffee breaks. There *is* more pressure, and as a consequence there is a greater need to take breaks from the pressure.

Those same people who discovered how many cows it takes to produce cream for our coffee undoubtedly would also be able to show us that efficiency and morale are higher because of a brief pause from the daily grind.

You and I need breaks from our routine, and twentieth-century man may not be able to find much happiness, or even survive, if he does not learn to cooperate with the natural rhythms of life—work and play, routine and rest, labor and recreation. There is, as Ecclesiastes says, "a time to cast away stones, and a time to gather stones together."

Without this rhythm whatever we do will run the risk of becoming stale, dull, or less creative. Too much work produces ulcers, heart disease, and frustration. Too much play produces indolence, parasitism, and a loss of dignity. Just as coffee drinkers are convinced that their imbibing forty-nine beans in each cup will give them lift and refreshment, so ought we to understand that recreation will help keep the race of life from becoming a rat race.

The coffee break may be, for some, a contemporary form of Christian communion. How many wounds have been healed, how many anxieties calmed, and how many angry attitudes transformed into friendly ones because persons shared coffee together can never be known. What can be known, however, is that real communion is a spiritual experience, and the fellowship of persons is more essential to the experience than a certain kind of beverage. Just as the first communion was a simple meal of commonplace ingredients, so can the coffee break be for modern Americans both a time of refreshment and a time for drawing closer to God by drawing close to one's fellow men.

Prayer: O God, our Creator, you who blessed work and dignified labor, help us also to feel your presence in recreation, rest, and relaxation. May our coffee breaks be times of communion with each other and with you. In the name of Him who went away from the crowds from time to time to rest. Amen.

On Seeing an "X" Movie

For a church member to attend the movies these days in
small- or medium-sized towns, special preparations must be
made. A disguise is probably necessary, such as dark glasses
and a false mustache, although on cold days a turned-up
collar and a hat pulled low may keep his identity secret. The
ability to change one's voice is helpful, although this is
necessary only when the box office girl might recognize you.
Once you are inside the theater, however, you will probably
not be discovered, as most of the audience is composed of
other church members, who don't want to be identified
either, and dirty old men whose eyes are glued to the wide
screen.

The reason for such discretion is the advent of the rating
systems for our movies. An "X" or an "R" rating is obviously serving as a means to publicize a film's pornographic
character under the guise of protecting the public. We are
witnessing the advent of pornography as an important and
much sought after box office attraction. Now, with our
naked eyes, we can witness every conceivable manner of
biological union—heterosexual, homosexual, or monosexual.

It's all there in technicolor, and the gross* profits from cheap "X" rated movies boggle the mind. The problem for Mr. Churchgoer as he sits slouched in his seat, trying to decide whether to risk removing his dark glasses, is made more complicated by the fact that there are "X" movies and then there are "X" movies. Every now and then a highly moral movie—indeed, even a Christian movie—is produced and given an "X" rating. The churchgoer may even admit to his spouse that he was physically present at such a show. More likely, of course, he will claim he read the review in *The Christian Century* or *Together* magazine, but temporarily, at least, his guilt feelings will disappear and he will feel cleansed once again.

Furthermore, one of the main things that is wrong with "X" movies is the "G" movie. People running around in the buff will get a movie an "X" rating every time, but *True Grit,* which approvingly tells the story of a vengeance-obsessed teen-ager and an alcoholic, corrupt law officer hunting down and killing bad guys who are only a little worse than they are, is regarded as "suitable for family viewing." "Vengeance is mine, saith the Lord," but revenge seems to be happily delegated to men when John Wayne plays the part and the American Legion gives it its blessing.

Congress, which seeks to exploit the pornography issues in the same way pornographers exploit sex, predictably seeks to help us guilt-ridden, church-going voters by appointing a commission to study pornography. Its tentative conclusion —wouldn't you know—was that "there was no evidence that exposure to pornography operates as a cause of mis-

---

* A particularly appropriate figure of speech.

conduct in either youth or adults." Which is to say that all those dirty movies don't really cause mass perversion in the streets.

It may be, fellow Puritans, that this is not the real reason why the private Christian, as he meditates upon his sins, has reason to be concerned. For the Christian who sees sex as a positive part of God's creation, for the men and women who are not ashamed of their sexuality, the striking thought is that the supersaturation by the media with sex may achieve the dubious end of making sex *dull*. Sex, good or bad, may become so commonplace that it will be as welcome as water to a drowning man.

Just about the time churches have freed themselves from their own hang-ups long enough to affirm that sexuality is good and positive, we're flooded with so much trash that many are starting to think sex is dirty all over again, and dirty sex invariably becomes uninteresting. Sex as a form of communion, as an act of love, as a testament of devotion, as an expression of joy between two people who consciously accept the responsibilities that accompany it—this kind of sex invests the relationship with meaning and excitement. Certainly it is seldom dull. Thus, in the quietness of our closets and the privacy of our souls, we find that our generation must face the temptations of sex familiar to all generations, in a new way. We need more wisdom than before to choose between trash and treasure. We need more honesty than before to rise above rationalizations justifying the time we spend watching and hearing intellectual and spiritual garbage. And, most of all, we need to demonstrate the tremendous personal responsibility which is necessary before sex, as practiced or thought about, will deserve God's blessing and approval.

Prayer: O Creator God, thank you for creating us as sexual beings. Forgive us, as a nation, for our preoccupation with sex, and forgive us, as individuals, for letting sex be our master instead of our servant. Give us common sense and good judgment when we go to the movies, that we may be able to discard our disguises and discover more of your truth. Strengthen the hand of the genuine artists who seek to serve mankind in the movies they make. May they get good reviews from us and from you. In the name of Him who knew the temptations of men. Amen.

On Having Two Children in 4-H

Of all the organizations in the world which teach our youth how to live responsibly and decently, none is better than 4-H. Boys and girls in both cities and towns not only learn how to sew, bake, and build, but they also learn how to work with other children and adult leaders at the same time.

Their parents learn a great deal, too—mostly about how to arrange their lives and everybody else's lives in the family to fit the 4-H schedule. If the 4-H'ers pledge their little heads, hearts, hands, and health, so do their parents, who soon discover that the involvement in such clubs demands commitment like unto that made by a Franciscan priest in a moment of emotional fervor.

For example, should a family desire to take a vacation together (a venture encouraged by all the better family magazines), it discovers that certain conditions must be met. The dog must also go along because she is being trained for the show at the county fair, and one week without training will undoubtedly damage her canine psyche beyond repair. Of course, 4-H meetings cannot be missed and are always carefully planned so that no more than four days separate them one from another. This is especially worrisome if, as is often the case, each of the children who is involved is committed to dog training *and* sewing *and* baking *and* ceramics *and* garden. The mother of the home is constantly going to or coming from a meeting, every one of which must be attended, for not to attend means black marks in the record book, a fate somewhat better than death by burning, but not much. The father spends his time waiting for supper which has been delayed because it interferes with the daughter's class in food preparation!

The family, one would think, would enjoy extra delicacies, such as the products of the baking program of 4-H. Not so. The family gets to "enjoy" only the mistakes, while the beautiful and probably delicious creations are carefully wrapped in cellophane, taken to a distant place, laid upon a table to dry out and be stared at, and returned home only when time and environment have combined to make them thoroughly inedible.

One would also assume that knowing how to sew would be a money-saving skill, which it is. *Learning* how to sew, however, is a stitch of a different pattern. True, on awards night the announcer relates, honestly, the cost of each garment, as in "Miss Milly Jones now models her dress made of combed cotton with hand-stitched doo-dads and perforated thingumabobs, costing only $2.98." The price is accurate *if* one does not count the cost of the several bolts of cloth consumed during the "experimental" period, nor the hours at the minimum wage rate spent experimenting, nor the cost of counseling required to soothe the troubled spirits of the entire family whose morale has gradually been destroyed. One could probably buy the same dress at Saks Fifth Avenue more cheaply.

Friends and relatives get to share in 4-H work, too, whether they want to do so or not. After all, how does one dispose of the several ceramic "things" which sons and daughters produce with their very own hands? The household can absorb only so many ceramic ashtrays, figurines, pin dishes, celery trays, finger bowls, and saltshakers. Thus, Aunt Mary can safely predict at least the general category of the gifts which she will receive at Christmas, for birthdays, and even on Groundhog Day, if the ceramics business has had an active season. A ceramic groundhog is clear evidence of a 4-H member in the family.

All these tireless efforts and threats to family stability are motivated by a few pieces of cloth called prizes. For those pieces of cloth, especially the blue ones, children will commit themselves to efforts that bribes, threats, or rewards of other kinds could not produce. Like Pavlov's dogs, their little mouths fairly water at the thought of receiving one; in turn, their eyes water when their efforts prove to be in vain.

Is this good? The answer is both yes and no, as is so often the case in real life. To the extent that prizes can become an end, rather than the satisfaction of doing the work itself, the competition is not worth the price. However, to the extent that children learn to accept responsibility and lose themselves in tasks outside themselves, it is clearly worth the cost. When, as is sometimes the case, children learn to share and bear the disappointments of their peers, as well as their own, such experiences teach the essential meaning of Christian love. To see a child—at an age when he is particularly self-centered and selfish—rejoice in another child's success (blue ribbon) and mourn his failures (white ribbon) whatever his own achievement has been is a thing of beauty. For in the long run it matters not whether you win or lose, but how well you learn to love each other in the process. For when that last great 4-H Record Keeper comes to write against your child's name, he will not record ribbons won or lost, but how well he loved his competition and how joyfully he participated as he played the game.

Prayer: *O God of all, who knows our inner thoughts and secret feelings, help us to see that our means must always be consistent with our ends. Help us keep our priorities in order that relationships will always be more important than blue ribbons. In the name of Him who is our final judge. Amen.*

On Growing Grass and Kids

In the spring a young man's fancy turns to thoughts of love, but his wife usually wants him to work in the yard. Working in the yard can be fun, especially when one seldom does it, or most especially when one hires someone else to do it.

The primary reason why Mr. American works in his yard is that he has been seduced by the pictures in *Better Homes and Gardens*. That magazine always shows a beautiful, finished yard with luxurious flowers, a carpet of lush, green grass, and a patio appropriate for the afternoon stroll of the Queen of England. What the editors of *Better Homes and Gardens* (who probably live on the thirty-second floor of a New York apartment building) do not show, however, is children—small, medium, and large children who are the natural enemies of flowers, grass, and patios.

Children love flowers, and so they often pull them up and give them to their parents. They have little personal animosity toward grass, too, but it is difficult to grow grass when three fourths of all the human population of a city either live in your block or walk across your would-be lawn on the way to their homes—if they have any. The dog usually sleeps in the sandbox where the children are supposed to play, while children haul the sand to the patio where it gets in the hamburgers the adults would otherwise eat, and the hose we turn on to water the places the flowers once were and the grass might have been is used instead to drench the children which, in the last analysis, may be the only living things that will be able to grow in such backyards. Additional discouragements include the attitude children have toward the actual process of groundskeeping and lawn care for which fathers and mothers feel some obligation. From a six-year-old child's point of view, what are leaves for that have been neatly raked into piles? For jumping into and scattering about, what else? Why trim the hedge? So that it can be used as a hurdle in a neighborhood steeplechase, of course. The purpose of spading the garden? Obviously, to find fishing worms.

In this, as in all things, fellow domestics, there is probably a message. Before a man can have peace of mind about his yard, he must make certain basic decisions. Does he want to raise children or grass? Are children more fun than flowers? In his more rational moments, of course, the average adult will choose what any experienced parent would choose: grass and flowers. However, we are not always rational and our emotions usually reign, so instead we choose children.

The point is, though, that once the basic decision has been made, some peace of mind can be experienced. The bare spot under the tree where hangs the tire swing can be accepted in the same way a bald spot on your own head can be accepted: with thanksgiving for that which still grows around it. The bird bath which now lies on the ground since its base, after four repair jobs, is broken and its pieces scattered makes an excellent meeting place for the dime-store turtles which might otherwise surprise you in your bath. What grass does survive, furthermore—after it has been trampled, squashed, plucked, mangled, and fed to guinea pigs—will mean more to you than White House lawns mean to presidents.

It has been said, in fact, that the neatly manicured, carefully nurtured and painstakingly massaged yard of today's suburbanite is a sign of his misplaced priorities. He doth care too much for his grass. We, too, need to consider the lilies of the field and how they grow. God knows our needs and he knows the needs of children. He knows—and we need to be reminded—that stewardship of life requires putting first things first and second things second—and last things last. Better kids than gardens, for remember the neatest lawns and the most beautiful gardens are usually found in cemeteries where children seldom play and the sounds of the living are conspicuous by their absence.

Prayer: *O God, we give thanks for noisy, active, grass-trampling children. May their spirit and enthusiasm capture us, even as they pick our marigolds and chase their dogs through the roses. Help us not to resent them but to rejoice with them. Help their parents to teach them good manners, but, more importantly, teach us forgiveness and the difference between what is important and trivial in our daily lives. In the name of Him who loved children. Amen.*

On Acquiring Guinea Pigs

More than one unsuspecting father has entered his home after a hard day at the office—or wherever his days are made hard—to be greeted by the patter of little feet heretofore unfamiliar to his ear. Usually such an event does not mean that a new baby has arrived at his address, as—contrary to the way in which the movie industry deals with pregnancy— the father knows about forthcoming children. Besides, *their* feet don't patter for a few months.

What such fathers discover, however, is a new and special kind of responsibility, a delightful creature, the darling of the kindergarten set, that bright-eyed and tail-less beast— the guinea pig. True, given his position as titular head of the house, it is somewhat surprising that the father knows nothing about the coming of the animals. Seldom is a father outvoted in family councils about whether or not to acquire such animals; the problem is that he is never seriously consulted on the matter at all. The wife (née: mother) *always* sides with the children in such matters, and it is vaguely implied that to reject a guinea pig is undemocratic at best and un-Christian at worst.

The father, as figurehead of the house, may try firmness and issue various ultimatums, including the old favorite, "either the guinea pigs go or I do!" However, after several minutes of silent indecision on the part of the other members of the family, it is usually wise to withdraw that particular ultimatum. For better or worse, as they say during weddings and other traumatic occasions, the guinea pigs are probably there to stay until they join that great big pet farm in the sky.

Guinea pigs are usually kept in large cardboard boxes in the kitchen, a fact of which state boards of health should quickly be made aware of, more precisely stated, *get wind of*. These animals eat a simple diet, although they show a special fondness for corn, carrots, apples, lettuce, cookies, and fingers. Capitalistic free enterprise being what it is, guinea pig owners can also purchase huge bags of guinea pig pellets which are dehydrated and compressed corn, carrot, apples, cookies, and fingers but which have the extra virtue of being expensive.

Guinea pigs also eat their boxes, their own little homes. This means that they often leave the kitchen to visit other parts of the house, including under couches, behind doors, and frequently in the beds of small children. In fact, it is fair to say that guinea pigs may have driven more young parents to their knees than has the need for prayer, although the need for prayer is more apparent when such animals are in the house.

This woeful tale has a happy ending, however, as the children usually outgrow their desire to possess guinea pigs shortly before group therapy for parents becomes necessary. In all honesty, too, the tale has a happy beginning and middle as well. For with all their many faults, the guinea pig has one overriding virtue which is sorely needed in a troubled and anxious world: he loves to sit quietly on a child's lap and be petted, stroked, and fondled. As an adult watches small children literally feed the ratlike creature huge doses of sincere affection, he gains an important insight into Jesus' directive that we should become as little children.

Who, other than a child, could really *love* a guinea pig? Possibly another guinea pig could, but we all know that animals are more loving than humans. Or, how many adults still have the capacity to delight in a chubby, squeaky, totally useless creature such as a guinea pig? Not many of us, my friends, are so disposed, and perhaps this is one of the reasons why the kingdom of God has not yet come in all its glory.

The problem, of course, is that we not only have difficulty in loving guinea pigs; we adults complicate much of life by insisting that the objects of our love be beautiful or expensive or prestigious. In a status-seeking world, where social pedigree seems to be the key to happiness, there is profound beauty in the love of a child for a pet or for any of God's creatures. Unless we become as little children—unless we become lovers of guinea pigs—we may not enter the kingdom of God.

Prayer: Dear Heavenly Father, we thank you for the world you have created. Help us not to judge guinea pigs as ugly or useless, or reject any part of your creation until we have seen it through the eyes of a child. Restore our innocence, so that our love might mature and become like Christ's. In the name of Him whose love embraced both man and beast. Amen.

On Filling Out Income Tax Forms

No ceremonial occasion is celebrated so universally with fear and trembling by the American people as is the dreaded tax deadline of April 15. It is at this time that one discovers how much of his total income goes to the United States government, and were it not for the fact that many people are refunded a portion of this sum, even the silent majority might rise up in revolution. It is at this time, furthermore, that John Q. Public learns how much he is really paying in interest on the house he is buying, how much (or little) he really gives to charity, and, in general, why in an affluent society he is continually broke.

He also experiences, should he choose to fill out the long form, one of the foremost occasions for frustration in the Western world. He can, of course, "cop out" and entrust his private affairs to H. R. Block and Company but should he cling to the myth of rugged individualism to the extent that he figures out his own tax payments, he can learn first-hand why the tax lawyers, rather than the meek, shall inherit the earth.

For one thing, no creation of man is probably more confusing or poorly conceived than an income tax form. This is not entirely the fault of those who write the forms, although they do what they can, as they must reflect the myriad of laws and non-laws that relate however vaguely to taxes. For example, consider out of context and in all its naked glory part of the instructions for figuring one's own taxes:

11. Tax Rate Schedule—

    a. If you itemize deductions, enter total from Part IV, page 2. If you do not itemize deductions, and line 9 is $5,000 or more, enter the larger of:

        (1)   10% of line 9 or:

        (2) $200 ($100 if married and filing separate returns) plus $100 for each exemption claimed on line 4, above.

    The deduction computed in (1) or (2) is limited to $1,000 ($500 if married and filing separate returns).

We humbly submit that such language is not easily grasped by the average man. Directions like these are clear only to certified public accountants, and it is sobering to remember that Al Capone got away with murder but was finally imprisoned for income tax evasion. The argument that the above language is now different is no argument at all, for part of the problem is that the forms are "simplified" each year, which requires a relearning process that complicates our ability to figure our taxes.

Consider, too, the dilemma of generous types who may seek to make contributions to worthy causes. Such gifts could be psychologically traumatic, if the donor is genuinely conscientious, and the taxpayer soon learns without realizing it what the apostle Paul meant by "condemnation under the law." For example, you are entitled to deduct the price of a cake given to a church bake sale, and the deduction is "the fair market value of the gift at the time of the contribution." If you do this, of course, you must "attach explanation" and be prepared to justify this donation if called before a tax inspector. (We can see it now. "Did you *really* donate that cake, Mrs. Jones? Did you make two cakes and only donate one? Tell me, Mrs. Jones, did your children lick the pan?")

If you deduct expenses for entertainment "for business purposes," is this legal if you enjoy yourself? Yes, we can deduct travel expenses while out of town "rendering services for a charity." But consider this dimension: what if you bought your wife a gift on the way home? What if, in fact, you knew before you left you were going to shop for your wife? What if, dear Christian taxpayer, you were planning from the outset to go shopping and you later decided to render a service for a charity?! What will you say about this when you face that Great Big Internal Revenue Service in the sky—or the one on the ground, for that matter?

Hidden beneath the legal jargon of the tax forms and concealed among the receipts you've saved for five years— which may get you a reduced sentence when your tax report is the one selected for random examination—we find a picture, in miniature, of the human condition. We can paraphrase Reinhold Niebuhr, who knew a lot about the human condition, to make this point: man's capacity for justice makes the income tax system possible; but man's inclination to injustice makes the Internal Revenue Service necessary. We are told that Americans demonstrate an amazing degree of honesty in filling out their returns—so much so that the system depends upon their honesty to work. We also see, if we can figure them out, the many checks and balances that there are in good old 1040. We learn, once again, that we are both good and evil, strong and weak, honorable and dishonorable.

We may also be able to see that we cannot save ourselves from this condition. No laws, however well written, can anticipate all the implications (loopholes) that the human personality is able to find. Form 1040 and its authors cannot save us. Thank God we do not have to justify ourselves before an omniscient God by filling out an Eternal Revenue Service form. We can rejoice in the fact that we are saved, not by the law, but by the grace of God.

Prayer: *O God who takes an interest in the affairs of men, help us to be honest men, even as we participate in the network of good and evil that is our civilization. Forgive us when we cheat, and forgive our government for its sinfulness in spending tax money for evil or selfish purposes. In the name of Him who said that tax collectors, and presumably taxpayers, can be justified if they repent of their sins. Amen.*

On Buying and Selling Houses

Those who have long felt that Jesus had no place to lay his head because of religious reasons may have to reconsider. It may well be that he simply couldn't make a deal with a realtor. Certainly his followers in modern times will have their faith sorely tested as they seek to serve God and buy a house at the same time.

Part of the problem is the exuberance with which realtors and brokers describe their houses. For example, if an advertisement says "You'll love the landscaping and the trees which surround the house," a prospective buyer will do well to check the foundation for cracks and the floorboards for termites. If it announces that it is priced "under $30,000," chances are it is on sale for $29,999.99. Should a house owner advertise that he is selling for reasons of health, it may mean that he has to go to Arizona for asthma, but it could also mean that he is sick of his crummy house.

When we were house-hunting on one occasion, a realtor told us he had a house within easy walking distance of our office, and technically he told the truth. It was "easy" walking, in the sense that there was no barbed wire to crawl under or hills to climb or rivers to swim. There was side-walk all the way—approximately two miles of it, to be specific!

We have learned to be careful in our responses to people who want to sell us a house because of its "potential," too. We examined one house, so described, which was well within our financial means. In fact, it was well within the means of almost anybody with the possible exception of a blind mi-grant worker on township relief. Its architectural style might have been described as early slum, and outside of needing a new roof, new wiring, new plumbing, new heat-ing, and a new foundation, only major repairs were required. In terms of "potential," there was no limit as to what could be done, since nearly everything needed fixing.

It is important, however, not to be exclusively critical of realtors and sellers of houses. Many times we inflict pain upon ourselves and produce anxiety by our own lack of reality. So many of us may discover a house we really "love" and regard as "exactly" what we wanted, but we immedi-ately want to knock out a few walls, remodel the kitchen, add a wing, and relandscape the yard. This is like buying the very ax that Abraham Lincoln used to chop wood, except that it has a new blade and a new handle.

Indeed, buying and selling houses is a major American business because one of the contemporary forms of man's finitude is his continual reaching beyond his grasp. People who can afford to live in $20,000 houses have mortgaged the next thirty years of their lives and hocked the family jewels to live in a $30,000 "dream house." The man who finally pays off the mortgage, shortly before retirement, goes into debt for a summer home which he finances by renting his other house to a couple who are renting their summer home to a family which is buying a winter home in Florida. We are a migrant people, in fact, for while we do not live in tents and trailers, we move from house to house because we are restless and hungry for that place where our dreams finally can come true.

The real danger, however, for the white, middle-class Christian is not that he will be gypped by a realtor or fail to find an appropriate place to rest his weary head. Instead, his danger is that he will be too preoccupied with his property and his possessions. Jesus warned us not to worry excessively about shelter and property, but, instead, to seek *first* his kingdom and his righteousness. It is fair to say, then, that the primary concern for the Christian ought not to be his *house* but his *home*. Houses can be bought or repaired or sold, but the warmth and love of a Christian home are not for sale. They can only be given away.

Prayer: Dear God, forgive our stubborn selfishness as we worry about mortgages, interest rates, termites, and damp basements. Help us to worry more about poor people who have no decent place to lay their heads and lonely people who have no families for a family room. Fill us with your Spirit so that our homes might be open to the world and our hearts to your inspiration. In the name of Him who was born in a stable. Amen.

On Learning
Generosity

Most of us who were born before, during, or within one generation of the depression are products of the Puritan ethic. To be a product of the Puritan ethic may mean that one does not "smoke or chew or go with girls that do," but it most often means that he is frugal with money. He saves for a rainy day or, in extremes, for the monsoon season while living in the Sahara.

We who represent such a background diligently nurture our children to be saving, to learn the value of a dollar, and to accept the God-given revelation that "a penny saved is a penny earned." In the writer's case, we first noticed that our economic puritanism had been absorbed by our daughter when she was two years old. That was the time when she thought she was a puppy dog and barked a lot.

At first, during the innocence of new parenthood, we thought the whole idea was cute. She was occasionally described as "adorable" as she crawled across the floor with her doggy bank in tow, saying "bowwow" all the while. Because we responded favorably to this by putting pennies in the bank, there occurred what behavioral psychologists call "reinforcement" and more practical people call "greed." She next put the touch on the grandparents, then the church secretary, and soon anyone who came to the house was greeted by a chubby little hand extended with the palm open and the doglike cry of "bowwow" or "woof, woof," our child's money call.

The situation soon became embarrassing, and we even made a public announcement in the church newsletter that church members were not expected to give her money, regardless of how hard she begged or barked. This announcement, however, did not reach the paper boys, the breadman, and the Avon lady, and when Sarah Lee saw their several well-filled purses, she shot around the corner faster than a greyhound, and barking like one as well. It was then that we finally gave up our permissive ways and applied some "negative reinforcement" to the seat of her diapers, as she had indicated that she might bite our friends on the legs should they refuse her. This would have been the final embarrassment, as she had not yet had her rabies shot.

The primary reason for this personal confession, however, is not to give young parents whose children think they are dogs the hope that this, too, shall pass. The primary reason is to remind the Christian family that the Puritan ethic of thrift is incomplete if training in *generosity* does not accompany it as well. Too many of us demonstrate a piggy bank or a doggy bank attitude toward money, but frugality can never be a substitute for charity in the Christian home.

Halford Luccock once commented on this very matter. He said: "In many, many homes Johnny is being given training in thrift and saving. I can just hear the proud parent saying, 'Put your nickels in the piggy bank, sweetheart! Listen, you can hear them: Ping! Ping! Ping!' Little Johnny and little Mary are being conditioned to like the ping! of a coin dropping into a china bank as if it were among life's sweetest sounds. So it is that the piggy bank helps the young financiers grow up into pigs. . . . If we provide a child with no other training in the use of cash, he may grow up to epitomize the little pig who stayed home, who never set forth on any adventure of giving, who never took part in any enterprise of service."

No doubt children will learn more from the *examples* of their parents in this matter than they will from any adult preaching or Sunday school picture lessons. Parents who want their children to grow into sharing, concerned, generous persons will simply have to be that kind of persons themselves. Some families teach both virtues at once, as they set aside a piggy bank where they save money to be used, regularly, for charity and worthy causes. Chances are, the attitudes they build within their children will deserve to be called Christian.

Thrift is fine, but generosity is finer. Christians ought to save for rainy days, but we should also remember that there are rainy days in the lives of some of our neighbors every day. Wasting money is wrong, but hoarding it for selfish reasons is just as wrong. There is, in short, the need for a thriftiness of generosity—the paradox which occurs when money is saved in order to be given on the rainy days of life.

Prayer: Heavenly Father, help us raise our children to be frugal with money. Help us to help them withstand the pressures of our society to buy useless and indulgent junk. Help us by our example to help them to be people of generosity, that we may show we're Christian by our love. In the name of Him who taught us that loving neighbors is like loving you. Amen.

On Riding the Subway

Most of the population of the United States now lives in cities. Living in the city has many advantages, as any New Yorker will tell you, for it is possible to enjoy cultural events, major league sports, and shopping advantages to a degree which underprivileged nonurbanites simply cannot have.

One such advantage which, from a country boy's point of view, urban dwellers can have as long as they would like is the transportation system of the city, a phenomenon which manifests a level of confusion and inefficiency outranked only by the Army and SDS. True, this writer's judgment is based on limited experience, but it should be made clear that his experience is limited for a sound reason: he once took a subway ride during the rush hour. The following account is slightly exaggerated, but this is merely—says a competent psychiatrist—the result of shock to the nervous system of city visitors which is often caused by subway rides at the rush hour.

It is not every day that we are squeezed, pushed, hauled,

jostled, jerked, buffeted, cursed, crunched, insulted, smashed, tangled, and elbowed in the groin within a thirty-minute period. At one point I was gripping a pole with all my ebbing strength—for what seemed to me to be a reasonable purpose, namely, to keep from being thrown out the door when the crowd was released from the car—only to discover that a sweet little old lady, who might remind you of your grandmother (if your grandmother is a professional wrestler!), was attempting to bend my arm the wrong way. She seemed to feel I was deliberately shoving it against her forehead, when in reality I was merely responding to a natural biological instinct for survival.

Unfortunately, I had no opportunity to explain my situation to her because of the two high school girls who had been sandwiched about me. They were determined to discuss their social problems rather loudly in my formerly good ear and with accompanying gestures which emphasized their main points but also succeeded in knocking my hat down over my eyes. For some reason this seemed to be a matter of some hilarity to them, although it merely widened the generation gap so far as I was concerned.

A generation gap was about the only unoccupied space in that particular subway at that particular time. Had I sneezed, someone else would have been able to share the experience—as well as dry my nose. As the car became more and more crowded with humanity, a small prayer of gratitude was expressed for Dentyne, Listerine, Ban, Scope, and all other products that take the worry out of being close.

It is somewhat shocking to realize that there were more people on that particular train than in the town where I grew up. It occurred to me, also, that the little man who sat through the entire trip under my left arm, soundly sleeping and totally oblivious to the noise about him, just might have been one of those strange itinerants in large cities who spend most of their lives in the subway—where you can ride forever and sleep and get off to shop or get a haircut or buy a meal. The shock is made greater by the realization that in New York City well over two million people ride the subways each day.

One message from all of this is obvious. Don't ride the subway during the rush hour if you can help it! However, a more significant point to be found in this experience is the realistic concern Christians must have about overcrowding this planet. Ours is a world in which there is rapidly becoming less and less space for each individual person. We are getting in each other's way, and the population explosion is not an abstraction that social scientists theorize about in sanitary laboratories. Where *are* we going to put our garbage? How long *can* we breathe the foul air we pollute? Where *are* all these people going to live?

Even more profound, and certainly more immediate, is the question of how are we going to relate to one another day after day? Any person who thinks he can live in peace without being conscious of another's rights and privileges needs to ride a New York subway. The final test of brotherhood will be when we are able to ride the subway day after day and arrive at our destination still loving the human race. Yet, this is our calling, to love people as children of God, on the subway or off, in groups or as individuals. The eternal command remains for us, even in the twentieth century: we love because He first loved us. Not even a subway ride at rush hour can change that command.

Prayer: O God of the cities and the towns, help us to love one another by finding ways to dispose of our garbage and being willing to raise our taxes to clean the air. Forgive us for what we have done to your world. Give us the resolve to clean it up, and in the meantime make it possible for us to live as brothers, even on the subway. In the name of Him who fed the five thousand. Amen.

On Losing and Gaining Weight

It has been said that only two things really concern the American people—how to lose weight and where to park your car. The subject of this meditation has to do with the former, for it is the greater barrier to spiritual wholeness.

Almost every person who has ever stepped on the scales has considered going on a diet. The evidence for this is the overwhelming interest in such matters the popular press has been demonstrating for years. "Sensible Diets You Can Afford" or "How to Lose Ten Pounds in Ten Days and Love It" are typical titles crying out to us poor overweight slobs who have difficulty reading the scales over those expanding barricades we call waistlines.

For a while, of course, we can rationalize our avoirdupois by pulling in our stomachs while we walk or by blaming the clothing manufacturers for not making seams as strong as they used to do. Or, we may remind our friends that fat men are jolly, or that, according to the insurance charts, we are not really overweight, we are simply four inches too short.

However, the day eventually comes when some occurrence convinces us that it is time we take off a few pounds. It may be seeing a photograph of yourself in a swimming suit or a smart remark by a teen-ager who may suggest that "we all take a couple of laps around Uncle Charlie for exercise." In this moment of truth we decide to forego our rationalizations, and to the momentary delight of our spouses and the skepticism of our children, we go on a diet.

Going on a diet is more easily announced than followed. Mark Twain supposedly said that anybody could quit smoking; he had done it dozens of times. Similar sentiments apply to dieting, as the most pleasurable part of diets is departing from them. The second most pleasurable part of dieting is talking about your diet with other people who may, or may not, be interested.

Indeed, conversations among dieters are often exercises in one-upmanship, as one dieter will seek to promote his diet or exaggerate his weight loss at the expense of the other. One dieter will begin with a claim of having eaten nothing but grapefruit and eggs for ten days, and his friendly opponent will parry with his steak and lettuce formula which helped him lose one more pound than the first person claimed. No persons in the world are quite such boors as dieters, and it may have been such as they who inspired Shakespeare to write the immortal lines, "Life [dieting] is as tedious as a twice-told tale vexing the dull ear of a drowsy man." (*King John*, III, 4.)

To the experienced dieter, however, all such conversation is understood for what it is—a cry for help. It is, again to quote Bill Shakespeare, so much "sound and fury, signifying nothing." Dieters talk about their weight loss and the special foods they eat and how many weeks they've been behaving themselves as a simple cover-up for the fact they're starving. They know what it's like to attend a party in which people are stuffing their faces with olives, peanuts, cake, and other calorie-laden goodies, while the guy living on grapes and Metrecal stands leaning against the wall, fighting his hunger pangs, and munching a chocolate-covered lettuce leaf. Only he knows how many different times he has slipped upstairs to the bathroom, stripped to his underwear, and weighed to see if any more of the "too, too solid flesh" (again, Shakespeare) has melted. Only he knows what it is like to be at a "plateau," a point at which it seems impossible to lose weight even if you eat nothing at all, run four laps a day around the block, and go to bed early to avoid temptation. How many times has he manipulated the scales, standing on one foot or gripping the molding around the bathroom wall in order to *seem* to lose a pound or two!

The purpose of this description of dieting and its pathos is not merely to invoke your sympathy, gentle weight watchers, but to direct our thoughts to higher matters. The Christian life is much like dieting in many ways. We look for shortcuts to the grace of God, just as some people long for crash diets. We show pride in our successes, but in the solitude of our closets (or bathrooms) we experience the self-doubt and anxiety of the troubled spirit. We hit plateaus in our lives when we seem to stagnate, when life is dull and uneventful.

Perhaps, too, the hard facts are the same in both situations. Christian living and dieting both require self-discipline and balance. If you want to lose weight, you must simply adhere to a plan that causes more calories to be used than are eaten. The Christian, too, must live the disciplined life, choosing his priorities with care and denying himself those things which are incompatible with a Christlike life. The Christian must balance the demands of self, neighbor, and God into an integrated whole, too, and there is simply no substitute for so doing. Finding the Kingdom is more difficult than losing weight, as worrisome as that is; but it is also more important and many times more rewarding.

Prayer: *O God, who knows our innermost thoughts, help us to find will power and self-discipline when we need them. Help us to recognize, too, that we cannot find your kingdom by our own efforts but only by accepting your grace and the free gift of your love. In the name of Him who understands our weakness. Amen.*

On Having a Disease

To be in seriously bad health is no laughing matter. However, to have a disease that is serious enough to warrant sympathy, uncommon enough to solicit interest, and complicated enough to make one the center of attention in groups can be a great blessing. Such a disease is sugar diabetes.

The author speaks from experience on this matter, for he had never been seriously ill in his entire life, never even having spent a night in the hospital on his own behalf, until he discovered in middle age that he was diabetic. The process of discovering it was not funny, it must be admitted. As one's vision clouds up, as weight loss comes faster than the most ambitious dieter could hope, and as person after person whispers behind your back about how bad you look, it can be a discomforting experience. Indeed, one can become more than slightly paranoid as friends offer to help you to a chair and your neighborly funeral director starts dropping over for coffee.

Nevertheless, once you've survived the diagnosis, accepted the reality of your situation, and begun to feel better, you discover that there are positive advantages to having such a disease. For one thing, it is a well-known fact that people do not like to receive shots with a hypodermic needle from anybody, and there is a special horror in giving such shots to one's self. To do this daily, then, is regarded as an act of courage not unlike leading the charge of the Light Brigade or climbing Mt. Everest. To make jokes about one's disease, too, only builds up the image of courage. ("My wife calls me Sucaryl heart instead of sweetheart. Ha! Ha!") No wonder strong men honor those of us who laugh in the face of death, and even our children reveal pride in their voices as they say, "There goes my dad."

Even more enjoyable, however, is the way in which a diabetic can dominate table conversations. All such conversations begin in the same way, as the diabetic soon learns to exploit the refusal of sugar for his coffee or the rejection of dessert while all others are accepting theirs. "Oh, are you on a diet?" "No, the ol' pancreas won't allow it." By interjecting the word "pancreas," one opens a whole new dimension of conversation about his disease, as amazingly few people are aware of the connection between diabetes and the pancreas. The diabetic is allowed, then, to discuss knowledgeably the whole range of his illness, from what causes diabetes through how the pancreas works to the hazards of insulin shock. Indeed, one can perform a noble service to mankind by sharing his illness, as nearly everyone has a relative or friend who is diabetic, and he is a tiny bit worried that he, too, might one day have to give himself shots!

During such conversations, it is best to treat the whole business in a matter-of-fact way. This enhances one's image of nobility ("How can he be so calm in the face of such a disease?"), but it also makes it possible to save face should, by coincidence, the diabetic find himself at table with some other person whose disease is *more* interesting than his. It is bad enough to discover another diabetic at his table, but this merely requires sharing the spotlight for awhile with a fellow sufferer. The real rub comes, however, when you find yourself in the company of one who has had open-heart surgery or gall bladder problems. Gall bladder types are terrible boors, as they don't eat butter, and this gives them an entrée into discussion which can frequently do real damage to a diabetic's dominance of the conversation. With practice, though, the diabetic should be able to overcome whatever bids for attention an appendix, hernia, or broken leg can claim.

In the solitude of the closet, however, the diabetic—or anyone who has a disease—discovers another danger which is best described by the vocabulary of faith. He can become so preoccupied with his own illness that he turns in upon himself. Instead of being a Pharisee who talks about his righteousness, he becomes a hypochondriac. He thinks the whole world should be interested in his blood sugar. We may even have to face the hard fact that the phrase "Christian hypochondriac" is a contradiction in terms.

Our health is important to us, certainly, and temperate, moderate living is required of us all. Still, to know God and to serve our neighbor requires a loss of self-righteousness and preoccupation with self. For what will it profit a man if he should dominate the whole conversation with his pancreas and still lose his soul?

Prayer: O Great Physician, help us never to exploit our diseases till we become pests to others and an embarrassment to ourselves. Quiet the secret anxiety we have about our health and give us energy and strength to match the tasks you have for us to do. In the name of Him who told a hypochondriac to take up his bed and walk. Amen.

On Going to the Hospital for a Checkup

To go to the hospital for major surgery is a traumatic experience for the patient and his family. Going for a comparatively "safe" reason, such as tests or a checkup, ought not to be such an experience. Why, then, is it?

The answer, as any patient, present or past, can testify, centers about the fact of the humiliation—the total, uncompromising, humiliation—that the unsuspecting patient undergoes. The probability is that the hospital staff does not conspire to humiliate or psychologically annihilate such patients; it only seems that way. Nevertheless, from the head surgeon to the intern, from the registered nurses down to the unregistered guy who cleans the toilets, there appears to be a united front, as all seem bent on reducing to absolute zero the confidence, sense of well-being, and reasonably stable mental attitude of the patient.

113

For example, persons in the hospital for checkups usually undergo a series of X rays. In and of itself, this ought not to be a major undertaking. However, the patient soon learns that getting prepared for X rays is less than uplifting, as certain preliminary events—we are told—*must* occur. One of these is temporary starvation. For many hours before the pictures are to be taken, the patient is allowed no bread, no meat, no vegetables, and certainly no ice cream. He is allowed, however, to drink small cups of a brownish concoction which tastes considerably like spoiled turnips and is designed to clean out one's bowels for photographing. It is at this point that the hospital is to be congratulated for the careful planning it exhibits in linking these two procedures together. Certainly the liquid destroys any semblance of appetite the patient might have brought with him to the hospital, and the effectiveness of the solution is so complete that the patient has no time for worrying about the forthcoming X rays, as he spends the subsequent twelve hours going to and from the nearest available bathroom. To and from. To and from.

These events, though, are merely the beginning of his dehumanization. Sustained by the hint that he may be allowed breakfast after the X rays the next morning, he soon experiences some of the psychological reactions observed in prisoners of war while they are held in concentration camps. The entire nervous system begins to deteriorate when he discovers that X rays scheduled at 8:00 A.M. are not really going to be taken before 9:30 A.M., and even then they are taken very slowly. Indeed, many a patient, as he lies stretched on the hardest table ever created by man, not quite dressed (for his X-ray gown has two ties missing in back), sees his whole life flash in front of his eyes, and he wonders if the X-ray technician really exists or if he, like Santa Claus, is only a figment of his imagination.

His fears are temporarily dismissed when a technician does appear, but they are replaced by new forms of anxiety as the pictures are taken. The reason for delay soon becomes obvious: the technicians have been studying the patient through peepholes in the wall, trying to discover his most vulnerable points. Should he have a sore hipbone, then by all means he must support his entire weight on its sorest point for ten seconds while an enormous machine hovers over his quivering body like a giant carnivorous bird. His body is twisted into positions only a professional contortionist would attempt; he is told to hold that position (without breathing!) until further instructions. The further instructions, of course, are to "resume breathing" and are given approximately three seconds before the patient turns purple.

The time spent waiting for the X rays to be developed is also calculated to reduce a man to trembling hands and garbled speech. For one thing, it always takes longer to read X rays than the doctor says it will take, and no one—absolutely no one—provides any information about you or your possible diseases in the interim. You are not left alone, however, as they keep checking your "specimens," taking your temperature, and pricking your finger. Laboratory technicians and X-ray technicians are evidently members of the same sadists' union, as they both seem to find pleasure in other people's pain. Lab technicians, for example, all use the same procedure for getting blood samples. It is called "trial and error," and it may just be the final blow—the *coup de grace*—in a patient's dehumanization.

All the above, while slightly exaggerated, is soon forgotten when the reports are finally revealed, and you discover that you are going to live a little longer with minor inconveniences, such as pills or shots. Or, if the news is bad, and surgery is necessary, the "suffering" of the tests is put into proper perspective. That which was "unbearable" somehow is quickly forgotten.

There is a message in this phenomenon which we can take seriously. Our aches and our pains are relative to our mental attitude toward them. We know hypochondriacs who seem always in the process of dying. To them, Christ said: "Take up your bed and walk. Get over your escapism. Be a full person." We also know people who carry authentic thorns in their flesh, who daily face great pain or serious handicaps with such a spirit of joy that they lift the hearts of other people. Blessed are they, for they help us know that God does not desert us in suffering. In a mysterious and miraculous way he enables us to live with pain and rise above despair. He is a great comforter, available to all who put their suffering into perspective and delight in whatever joys of life still call out to them.

Prayer: O Christ, who challenged the neurotics to stand up and walk, who knew the suffering of the cross, and who calls us to life, not death, help us to rise above the temptation to enjoy our pain and give us grace for living in a world where great suffering surrounds us. In the name of Him who suffered for our sake. Amen.

On Sending a Daughter to College

Sending a child to college has long been a traumatic experience for parents. For most parents it is the first really major separation of themselves from their sons and daughters, and all parties involved see this occasion as the most significant cutting of the umbilical cord to have taken place up to this point in their lives.

So it has always been, but in recent years sending one's child to college has assumed terrifying proportions. Each day during the school year, it seems, the news media are reporting a new crisis on campus or exposing a new vice among students. Will their children, parents wonder, one day soon be taking over the president's office? Will they be marching with hundreds of their peers to protest the food service on campus or the closing of the city parks at midnight? Or will they become hippies, with hair down to their shoulders, grubby clothing, and a general appearance similar to something that crawled out from under a rock?

The anxiety parents feel is demonstrated in a variety of ways. One such way is that of wanting the college to assume the role of *in loco parentis,* a phrase that is well known to most deans, hated by students, and embraced by parents as meaning "to watch over" their children. Parents will write letters, hinting that it would be nice if the Dean of Women would evaluate the boy their daughter is dating, finding and sharing information as to his religious beliefs, moral standards, loyalty to the United States, appearance, vocational goals, and academic abilities—without, of course, raising any suspicions by the boy or girl.

Colleges respond to this anxiety in a variety of ways. Some colleges adopt extremely strict rules and regulations and enforce them by employing a number of monitors, head residents, and supervisors. This is very comforting to those parents who regard college as a kind of coeducational nunnery, and it is educational for the students, as they devise warning devices and procedures for beating the system which demand their best intelligence and most ingenious ideas.

Other colleges face the problem squarely and seek to be realistic as to what freedoms students may have and what rules parents can cling to for hope. Thus, should it become the vogue among students to have, say, coeducational nudist parties in which the young ladies and gentlemen get together to play chess, checkers, and other games, the college will respond by not allowing checkerboards on campus! This means that the students will regard the administration as liberal in that it does not seem to object to student nakedness, and brings comfort to parents who know how corruptive checkers can be.

Most threatening to parents, however, is the realistic fear that the *ideas* of their children may change. Will their little

Susie come home for Christmas vacation believing in free love, advocating the legalization of marijuana, and spouting slogans favoring recognition of Red China in the United Nations? Will she become an atheist? Even worse, will she believe in God *too much* and become a fanatic and want to be a social worker in the slums? This is why parents weep when they depart from the college of their daughter's choice and leave her behind. (It is also why the faculty and administration, in whose care she has been left, cry a lot, too.)

This writer, who has been a Dean of Students and who entrusted his daughter to the care of another college, knows and understands these feelings. He doesn't know what to do about them, but he recognizes them when he sees them. Prayer has been helpful in bringing peace of mind temporarily, but this has not proved to be a totally effective way of establishing such things as dormitory policies, for which there is little biblical precedent.

Actually, separating one's self from his child when he leaves her behind at college is not the time to pray for a miracle or guardian angel (translation: Dean of Students). At this point, to be candid, one must ask some direct questions and accept the consequences of his answers. Are we ready to let our children go? Do they enter college with a faith strong enough to withstand criticism and its challenges? Are we really able to communicate with our children? Can they be honest with us?

Because we love our children and wish the best for them, releasing them for college in times like ours is a sobering responsibility. We find our own faith is tested, as well as that of our children. And we, like them, may rapidly learn our human limitations and place greater dependence upon God's help than ever before.

Prayer: O God, help us to stay close to our children as they are growing up, so that when they leave us we can let them go without irrational fears. Be with those people at college whose influence over our children is so great, and help parents to be equal to the tests which lie before them. In the name of Him who worried his parents when they left him at the synagogue. Amen.

On Returning to College for the Fifteenth Reunion

College reunions are advertised as glorious occasions for keeping in touch with the old school, for seeing old buildings, cheering the fighting team to victory over the old enemy, and seeing old friends once again. They are billed as elaborate exercises in nostalgia, planned with scientific precision by the Alumni Office with close cooperation (this is significant) from the Development Office.

All colleges want happy alumni, and nothing warms the director's heart quite so much as the letter which begins, "My whole life was changed at good old Siwash," especially when it concludes with the words, "Enclosed is a check for. . . ." The more letters, testimonies, and public statements which include the phrase "good old" that can be inspired, the more checks the Alumni Office can anticipate.

College reunions and homecomings are calculated affairs, set up to invoke as many warm feelings around the heart as possible and carefully planned to screen out any pains or bad memories which might otherwise be experienced.

Thus, dinners are always scheduled for former athletes to get together under the sponsorship of the Lettermen's Club. The agenda for such meetings varies from school to school, but all have one necessary event in common: the opportunity for lying about past athletic achievements. This is why the members of the school's undefeated team of 1931 will be honored. It provides an occasion for overweight old grads to update their achievements on the gridiron, for as memories get fuzzier and eyewitnesses fewer, the big game gets bigger and so does "Killer" Jones's role in it. Indeed, if a man makes the second team while in college, we can be sure he will have been a varsity member by the time he is twenty-five, an all-conference selection by age thirty-five, and all-American by retirement.

College reunions are also exercises in one-upmanship. Persons who have turned out to be failures seldom return for alumni occasions, and those who plan the events will certainly not seek them out (we undoubtedly will never experience an introduction by the Alumni Director as follows: "Here is John Jones, class of 1944, who is now a beachcomber!"). Thus, those who return for homecoming or alumni day often engage in the subtle game of "image projecting." This is done by looking prosperous, in terms of dress if one is in business, or tweedy and intellectual if in the arts or education. Phrases such as "John is on the road all the time now that he is head of sales" or "Our sabbatical last year in Greece was just dreadful" abound in alumni conversations. So do those terrible little sentences which are uttered as two old grads meet, find it impossible to remember each other's names, and stubbornly refuse to admit the fact. ("Well, how are you, you old son of a gun?" "Fine. Say, you've put on a few pounds." "Yeah, a few since we cheered for Old Blue.") The conversation goes on ad nauseum, a fact which has made the name tag business one of the fastest growing industries in America today.

No one can really be blamed for this state of affairs. The Development Office must deal in nostalgia if it expects to retain the loyalty of the alumni, and some strategy must distract the old grads from the sight of the barefoot students who delight in dressing their shabbiest on homecoming, and insist upon taking a motorcycle apart as close to the registration table as possible. The alumni themselves are merely indulging in an expression of their own humanity, as life in the world can sometimes only be endured when we exaggerate a little in front of others who honor the rules of gamemanship.

Homecoming, though, teaches us some important moral and spiritual lessons, if we can achieve that difficult stance of looking at ourselves objectively. We may, upon seeing again an old girl friend we once "loved" but didn't marry and upon noticing her double chins and extra pounds, believe once again in the grace of God. We may also be sobered by the knowledge that she may well be thinking the same thing!

However, the important truth is that we can't really go home again. We can't live in the past or recapture distant memories. The good old days at college never really existed. We created them because they make the present more enjoyable, even bearable, and a return to the alma mater really calls us back to reality. It reminds us of ideals since forgotten, resolutions long ago broken, and a time in life which can be remembered, albeit badly, but never reclaimed.

It is always good to *try* to go home again, for it reminds us we have new homes, new lives, and new duties to perform. We are called to live in the future more than in the past, for the God who rules the world is dynamic, not static, and it is always better to live with hope than to dwell upon yesterday's dreams.

Prayer: O God of the world, help us to see visions of the future beyond the dreams of the past. Keep us alive all of our lives, so we can enjoy yesterday without becoming enslaved to memories. In the name of Him who was and is and always shall be. Amen.

On Graduation

When we graduate from high school, chances are a digni-fied person from an important place will come to the school as a commencement speaker. Among other things, he will inevitably say that we are about to go out into the world, and the future will be in our hands. Should we graduate from college, chances are another prominent person will visit the school and say, in more words than are necessary, that we are about to graduate and go into the world where the future will be in our hands. Should we get an advanced degree from still another institution, probably another more prominent person will speak, making the point that we are about to go out into the world, etc., etc.

This recurrent theme of commencement speeches is a worthy one, but it does leave a fuzzy impression as to where the world is into which graduates are to go. The fact is that to be "in the world" means to be on your own, and all of life is a process of entering the world to a greater and greater degree.

We probably start being "in the world" as infants when we discover that crying leads not only to food, dry pants, and a burp job, but eventually to the simple satisfaction of being fondled, cuddled, and babied. We enter the world to some extent when we are allowed to cross the street by ourselves. We go even farther into it on our first day of school. Indeed, one of the more moving scenes in this writer's life was the sight of our second daughter bravely going hand in hand with her sister to her first day in school, clutching her teddy bear for all she was worth.

The first date is another big step into the unknown, as is the first kiss and the first hug. They are momentous occasions, for these events are comparable to opening a jar of olives: after the first one, the rest come easily.

When a boy or girl gets a driver's license, the world opens up for him or her in a way that it had not to that point. Nothing, in fact, is quite so anxiety-producing to many parents as the knowledge that their sixteen-year-old son is out in the dark of night driving a car that isn't paid for, with a girl they scarcely know, to a drive-in theater to see a movie about drag racing.

Mothers almost never approve of the way their daughters wear their hair. Yet, the time *does* come when a female young person has the *right* to fix *her* hair, and it is then that the mother of the world will hear the declaration of independence: "Please, Mother, I'd rather do it myself." In short, one does not go into the world overnight, like a chicken hatching from an egg. We enter the world in bits and pieces, through the process of little decisions and big ones, by gradually assuming responsibility for one's own actions.

Having said all this, it is necessary to be realistic about the fact that graduation represents entrance into the world in a special way: the *world recognizes your coming*. At about this time, the graduate will seriously evaluate the person he has been dating, not just in terms of his or her looks, charm, and personality, but in terms of suitability for marriage. In many states girls and boys can get married at eighteen without parental permission, and in all states people over twenty-one can satisfy the urge to merge without asking Pop or Mom. Uncle Sam, whom most schoolboys and undergraduates probably felt didn't really care, suddenly takes an interest in their bodies, minds, and—unfortunately—their souls.

At about this time young people learn that they can buy booze legally in most states and illegally in others. "X" rated movies are now theirs to enjoy, if that is possible, and they no longer will have to lie about their ages at the box office. Their fathers may confront them, as they stand under a tree after commencement exercises, with the comment: "Don't just stand there; start supporting yourself." They can vote, a much-anticipated event in the lives of students, and they now have the adult freedom to choose among several juvenile candidates who appeal to the basest instincts of voter-man.

Here, fellow graduates, is the point! The way we handle our freedom is what really determines whether or not we are ready for the world. Someone has said that there are only two kinds of people: those who are part of the problem and those who are part of the solution. Do we think only in terms of ourselves—how much we can take, what we can get out of life? Those who think that way are definitely part of the problem. Or are we concerned with the contribution we can make—how much we can give, how much we can put in? People like that are part of the solution.

This, then, is the basic choice that we are continually being asked to make. This is the choice which, as the saying goes, separates the men from the boys, the women from the girls, and—in a real sense—the Christians from the pagans.

Prayer: *O God, help us make wise decisions which are also moral ones. Help us see that we are all part of the problem some of the time, and part of the solution the rest of the time. Help us keep our parts in the right proportion. In the name of Him who set the standard for us all. Amen.*

On Going to Church

For many years and for many people, the act of going to church has been a routine experience. While denominational differences have led to a variety of worship services, most Protestants could count on a sermon, three hymns, some prayers, and an offering. Roman Catholics became accustomed to Latin Masses which they couldn't understand and a liturgy which most assumed would remain basically unchanged until the end of time.

Not so today. For good reasons or bad, the old-time religion has been modernized, and many a gentle parishioner of our time enters church each Sunday with fear and trembling, wondering what new devices will erupt to shock him and what new forms of word and event will be tried in the clergy's ongoing attempt to "communicate" with him. Will it be folk songs again, and will he have, one more time, to figure out the deeper meaning of Bob Dylan's mumbling? Remember when all sermons had an introduction, three points, and a poem? Now, if a sermon as such is included, it will perhaps be in the form of a dialogue or in bits and pieces from the mouths of several people popping up from the pews.

Or, he may be treated to the sight of several young girls

in leotards, dancing out the liturgy to the accompaniment of two bongo players in blue jeans. Swearing used to be on the "no-no" list everywhere and certainly in church. Now, infrequent profanity, if it makes a point, is acceptable, and one may expect at least one cuss word per month in city churches, and more if they are Episcopalian. Psychedelic lights, stereophonic sounds, root beer and potato chips in place of Communion, a miniature electric chair instead of a cross—these and other delights await the churchgoer who obviously needs more relevance in his symbolism. Only the offering plate remains the same.

Perhaps most unsettling are the new translations of scripture and the prayers that don't sound like prayers. Having been exposed to the New English Version, the Cotton Patch Version, or a Phillips translation, he may be prepared to withstand, from time to time, various youthful versions, as illustrated by the following "translation" of the twenty-third Psalm, appearing here in print for the first time anywhere:

The Man Upstairs is the Sheep-keeper;
I am with it.
He makes me sack out on the lawn.
He leads me by the quiet pond, and peps up the inner man.
He leads me down the straight and narrow to keep his
    name clean.
Even though I stroll through the graveyard scene,
It doesn't bug me,
For we're in it together and your hot rod and your stick,
They're the most.
You spread the cloth before me even in Squaresville.
You plaster the dandruff, my mug spills.
Yea, man, the most and the best shall dog me till the daisies
    sprout,
And I shall roost in Endsville till chickens lay square eggs.

Obviously, when such translations are compared with, say, the King James Bible, we can see how important it is to communicate in the idiom of the day. Yet, fellow church-goers, in the search for ways to communicate the gospel, there is a terrible temptation which confronts us all. We face a double risk, either horn of which may keep us from experiencing the worship we seek.

On the one hand is the temptation to think that worship only occurs when done in traditional ways and according to long-standing custom. God, some think, spoke in King James English, and if it was good enough for Peter and Paul, it ought to be good enough for us. On the other hand, there is the temptation of faddism. That which is contemporary is good; that which is new communicates; and that which shocks is the gospel. If it's good enough for Peter, Paul, and Mary, it's good enough for us.

The truth is, of course, that worship of Almighty God cannot be manipulated or guaranteed, whatever the format. Yes, gimmicks and clever techniques (whether old or new) can sometimes attract large numbers, but corporate worship is not synonymous with the presence of crowds. It can even happen for some and not for others at a given worship service, and we are all better for having the honesty to make such an admission. Whatever means we use to provide a setting in which the worship of God can occur, we run the risk of letting our own pet devices and prejudices interfere with the richness of the opportunity.

Perhaps the best we can hope for is the assurance that where two or three or more are gathered together, He will be in the midst. We're never sure how or why, but his promise can be enough to encourage us to run the risk.

Prayer: O God, who can be reached by men but never manipulated by them, forgive us for trying to put you in our little boxes. Forgive us for thinking that addressing you as "thee," or thou as "you," will show we are in touch with Almighty God, the Ground of our Being, the Father of Jesus Christ. Help us to be still and hear your voice instead of a playback of our own pet ideas. In the name of Him who called you Father and meant it. Amen.

On Not Going to Church

Nearly every calendar predicts that June, July, and August will follow the month of May—usually in that order. Nearly every minister who has worked in a church longer than one year predicts that church activity will follow a certain pattern during those same months; namely, that there will be about as many persons at the regular church services as there would be members of the Ku Klux Klan at a tea honoring Adam Clayton Powell for distinguished service to his country.

True, the annual exodus is easily justified. All have heard—or made the comment—that we can worship God on the golf course or by the flowing stream as well as, or better than, in the stuffy confines of a church building. In our mind's eye we can visualize little groups of golfers, kneeling at the fourteenth green for prayer, or a tennis player quoting from Genesis at match point: "And Joseph served in

133

Pharaoh's court." We recall, too, that some of the disciples were fishermen, and it is reasonable to be like them.

Nevertheless, even the younger ministers who are interested in depth and relevance and denounce statistics worry about high absenteeism in summertime. One even claimed to have had a vision about the problem, a vision informed by Isaiah 6:1-8 and more than likely related to his having eaten a pizza (with anchovies) at 1:00 A.M. before going to bed. While he was not completely coherent in the retelling of the vision, the following is at least true to the testimony as we have it:

In the year that my sister-in-law's hair was dyed, I saw a great congregation gathered in the pews, and many in the balcony, high and lifted up; and the members filled the temple.

Above the sanctuary sat several families; each had children, two of whom covered their faces during the sermon, and two of whom covered their ears, and two drew.

And a voice called, "Holy, Holy, Holy is the Lord of Hosts; the whole church is full of people."

And the foundations of the walls shook at this sound, and the room was filled with smoke. And I said: "Woe is me! The furnace has finally exploded and I am lost; for I am a Methodist, and I dwell in the midst of Methodists, and yet I have seen a church full of Methodists in the summer! Then one of the children came up to me, having in his hand a twenty-dollar bill he had taken with tongs from the collection plate. And he touched my hand with it and said: "Behold, this proves the loyalty of the Methodists; your cynicism is taken away and your pessimism about summer attendance is forgiven."

And then I heard a voice saying, "We need a loaf of bread and a quart of milk. Whom shall I send, and who will go for us?" Then my wife said: "Here I am. Send your father."

Certainly only a few mystics experience such visions, and it obviously does no good to complain about church attendance, since it makes little sense to preach about it to people who are present. Besides, we *need* to get away from our regular routine from time to time. Everybody knows that.

Two truths, however, deserve our consideration. One is the often overlooked knowledge that the God of both the Old and New Testaments was, indeed, frequently worshiped in the wilderness, without any seeming loss of power and effectiveness on his part. The worship of God can take place at other times than at 11:00 on Sunday morning and in other places than within the hallowed walls of St. George's by the Drive-In. The cause of Christian worship would, in fact, be greatly advanced if absentee members would simply stop apologizing for their absenteeism and transform the home, golf course, boat, or bowling alley into a place for private devotions. So long as public resources are not tampered with, even Madalyn Murray O'Hair would not complain.

The other truth is the reminder that *corporate* worship is essential to the Christian life. Worship in a boat is fine, but until the boat is big enough to hold a small congregation, whatever private devotions are practiced will not be sufficient. If we are strong, our strength needs to be shared with those who are weak. If we are weak, obviously we need the help of the corporate body.

In other words, getting out to church is not the question. Instead, we are called to be a part of the body of Christ, and no one can be a part of his body in isolation. We can do without the church part of the time, and some parts of man's version of Christianity we can do without all the time. But he who would know God personally will find the need, again and again, to share the burdens of others and the strengths of some in corporate worship—even in the summer.

Prayer: O God of all the seasons help us to find refreshment in your church as well as in your world. Forgive our lies about why we miss church and help us be close to you wherever we are. And keep us close to each other. In the name of Him who was always close to his Father. Amen.

On Running for Public Office

For many years now, pastors have been urging their congregations to enter public life, to become involved in politics, and to get other Christians to do the same. This is good advice, brethren, and we hope many Christians take it seriously. It is important, however, to make clear that such adventures are not without their risks, and one should know the dangers involved.

Humbly, this writer would like to share his experience with you, in the hope that you will run for public office anyway. What is written here is only a caricature of what really happened, and it concerns simply an election to a local school board in a small city. Furthermore, please weigh the fact that the writer experienced the mixed blessing of actually being elected, a turn of events that greatly helped his prayer life during his term in office.

You may have wondered why so many persons who run for public office resort to vague generalities in their campaigns and take forthright stands only in opposition to earthquakes, sin, and tuberculosis. Partly, of course, the reason is that the candidates want to win votes without making specific commitments, but the rest of the reason is that the people seem to want private miracles on public money.

What the public wants for its tax dollars from school boards can be summed up in two words: Nearly Everything. Many patrons would like bus transportation for all pupils, door to door, with no more than five-minute rides for any child. A full staff of teachers should be provided, of course, all of whom have Ph.D. degrees. Furthermore, they should be willing to work fourteen hours each day, keep abreast of educational developments in their fields by going to school each summer at their own expense, and cheerfully accept $3,500 salaries.

Many taxpayers also would like two new grade schools yesterday, a practical arts building today, and an auditorium tomorrow, all of which are to come about by reducing the cumulative building fund and lowering taxes. It will also be helpful if all members of the school board are thirty-five years of age with forty years' experience. Furthermore, each board member should have at least four children, one fifth of whom should be black to correspond to the racial distribution of the community.

Superintendents and principals should be men and women who are without sin and who possess infallible judgment. They should not, however, concern themselves too much with education, as a certain unknown but large proportion of school patrons will judge the success or failure of the entire system on either the win-loss record of the basketball team* or the number of honors captured in state contests by the marching band.

* Substitute "football team" where relevant.

Individual patrons, of course, will become very concerned about pure education when their sons or daughters fail to be accepted, with scholarship aid, into the college of their choice—even if their IQ ratings total 84 (sometimes for the entire family) and they failed drivers' training twice because they weren't used to a manual shift car. At all other times, though, school board members will be free from harassment, unless the subject of prayer in school comes up, a topic which causes a board member to be labeled a communist subversive if he's against it or a religious fanatic if he's for it.

All this having been said, it is important to see the lesson that such circumstances teach us. One does not have to run for or be elected to a school board to see an analogy with his own feelings in the above caricature. Anybody who sits on the side of a desk from which he has to make decisions which will spend public money in some ways and not in others, or delight some citizens and disappoint others, or honor some requests and reject others will experience the special frustrations of his position. He will feel put upon, misunderstood, unfairly treated, and hated by the rest of mankind. His frustration will cause him to sleep many nights in the prenatal position with the electric blanket turned up to nine.

So what else is new? People who would seek to follow Christ in their daily lives and expect to find their decisions easy ones, with clear-cut black and white choices, are naïve. The Christian in public life will simply have to keep his priorities and his goals in mind, for he will find himself in uncharted territory much of the time. His task is to blend worthy goals with possible means, and to be willing to compromise without being compromised. And he will need to seek forgiveness some of the time, too, both from God and man, for neither his faith nor his dedication will keep him from colossal mistakes and the temptation to justify them. Even so, Christ still says, "Follow thou me."

Prayer: *O all-powerful God, help us to use what power we have with humility. Help us not to become cynical or too sure we have all the answers. Keep our feelings from being hurt, and when we are set upon by citizens, help us to keep our cool. In the name of Him who was crucified. Amen.*

On Publishing
a Book

The uniqueness of every person is most clearly seen in what he wants out of life. Some men desire riches, others fame, and still others power. A few want to be rich, famous, *and* powerful, and a very few want only to retreat to a small cabin on a large lake—there to fish quietly all the days of their lives.

The writer of these words once felt that the publication of a book would satisfy his deepest needs. To see his words in print—ahh, such ecstasy could scarcely be imagined—and if this, only this, could be achieved, life would be worth living, and he would be ready when the time came to take his place in that great big writers' conference in the sky.

In this, as in all such dreams, the reality of the situation has a way of tarnishing things. To begin with, publishers, who play a rather central role in the entire process, have a gentle way of dealing with would-be authors which makes a two-year sentence to prison seem like fun. For one thing, your "book" is never referred to as a "book"; it is always a "project" or a "manuscript." The word "book" implies a finished product, and it is evidently necessary to make very clear in a variety of subtle ways that you are still a long way from writing a book even after you've written a number of pages, titled them, and sent them to the publisher.

The publisher will then farm out your "project" to a reader in whose hands your fate as an author rests. Readers are never identified, as anonymity is protected at all costs. Their phones are undoubtedly unlisted, which makes little difference because their names are known only to their spouses. Some writers even harbor the suspicion that all readers are single because no other person would marry such a cruel, analytical, calculating creature. After he has destroyed some of the great prose of our time with his blood-red pencil and undone some of the finest ideas of this century with his criticism, he probably will offer helpful suggestions, such as rewriting the first chapter, eliminating the second chapter, shortening the third chapter, and adding a final chapter. This is like jacking up your car and sliding in a new frame!

The publisher, on the basis of what his readers say, may run the risk of producing your near-book, if practically everything is changed in it. Or, the would-be author may get another letter which reads as follows: "We have read your manuscript with care and while it has much to commend it, it does not meet our publishing needs at this time." Translation: "We aren't going to publish your book, fella, but we're trying to be nice about it."

Should you eventually get it published, however, you soon discover that the rest of the world is less excited over this fact than you are. This is communicated by the fact that many bookstores do not carry your masterpiece at all, and those that do seldom put it in a prominent place with a red light shining down upon it, accompanied by choral music in the background. Friends, too, seem less than overcome by your authorship, and even the most interested ones say wrong things, for example, "Could you loan me a copy?" or "Is it in the library yet?" or "When will it be out in paperback?"

Not many journals review your book, either, and those that do usually simply quote three sentences from the preface, the title, and the names of the chapters. Occasionally, someone from a faraway place will write you a letter about your book, but it is usually a negative one in which your faith as a Christian or virility as a man is questioned. So humiliated are you by this time, however, that any kind of interest in your book is welcomed, as you have now been reduced from a starry-eyed optimist to a grim-lipped masochist.

Little joys and tiny beacons of hope for future glory sustain you, however, and a few nice things are said. Some seem nice only when compared to past disappointments, such as, "My brother-in-law read your book." Other genuinely nice comments are made in writing, such as the one this author received: "I found your book both creative and stimulating. I am recommending it to many people and I hope you sell thousands of copies. Love, Mother."

The point? In a way it is the same point that this entire book has been trying to make: whatever our goals, whether reached or not, one commandment must always be observed: Take not thyself *too* seriously, for only God is aware of our hidden talents and he *is known for forgiveness*.

Prayer: Dear God, help us to take ourselves less seriously than we do. Help us to set worthy goals for ourselves, but if we reach them, keep us from being boors. And if we fail to reach them, help us to remember that both we and the world may be better off. In the name of Him who wrote only in the sand. Amen.